REMOVING THE
MASK

Althea Clarke

Rehoboth Publications

REMOVING THE MASK

Rehoboth books may be ordered
through Amazon.com and other
booksellers.

Althea Clarke
Removing the Mask

ISBN-13: 9781795196666

Printed in the United States of America

DEDICATION

I dedicate this book to Jesus Christ my Lord and Savior who is the lover of my soul.

To my children, I love you all, you need to know I don't regret any of you. If I had to start life all over and you weren't with me, I would search all throughout the world to find each of you.

To my mother, thank you for giving me the opportunity and the chance to be where I am in my life, without you none of this would be possible.

Most of all my sweet nieces who have brought me through this journey with their support and patience and have stuck by my side no matter how difficult this book was to write. For they have seen my potential this whole time. To my confidant Mr. Jay you have looked after me more than half of my life and you are an angel sent from God. Thank you for being in my corner and making me feel special no matter what.

Jessica Dale, for believing in me. Natasha Grant for always being there to pick up my pieces. To all my brothers and sisters for being who they are, I wouldn't change you for the world. To the man Mr. Odeon Powell, that has made me want more for myself and be better. For it takes a strong man to make a strong woman. All the love and gratitude to you.

Thank you to Marguerite Breedy Haynes for believing in my voice and helping me to turn it into so much more. To anyone that has helped me on this journey, I thank you sincerely and dearly.

~

Contents

"Life is very interesting... in the end, some of your greatest pains, become your greatest strengths."

Drew Barrymore

1

The Beginning

I was born in Jamaica Parish of St. Mary's, a little tiny place in the Jamaica. Most people don't know of it, but the Jamaican Artist Capleton put it on the Map (SAYING ST. MARY'S ME COME FROM).

I was the oldest sister of four siblings surrounded with plenty of cousins, aunts and uncles. I remember the danger I would feel as a little girl and I can't seem to explain it but I was fearful of the culture there. It just felt unnatural to me and I am not sure as to why.

I hated funerals and the way they celebrated an individual's death. How I hated to lose a member of our family! The smell of evil, the fear of wondering if I will ever get out of there and not knowing if there was anywhere else to go.

All I can remember is the sadness of that tiny little place, the struggles and uncertainty. I have had some unrealistic feelings about our people and their culture, and from childhood, I seemed to have buried those thoughts and feelings inside.

When I relocated to Canada, I seemed to have the same feelings and dislikes that I did from the Caribbean Community and the same belief about them which is that they are full of self-hate and somewhat evil people.

Not every Jamaican is like that but in my experiences, I find that they are the only race of people that have devalued me and each other. They refuse to uplift each other, especially the women. They are not good to each other and I am not sure if they are good to themselves.

I have had the same feeling my whole life and it never went away. My entire life, I have buried the feelings I had and I didn't realize where the feelings were coming from. I put up a block in my mind for the last 40 years and was trying to be accepted by a race and a culture that do not even like each other or value themselves.

As a child I saw mothers and fathers beating their child with a machete, a stick, a bat or whatever they thought was necessary to do the job. They called it discipline or culture. Talk of spirits, black magic and all kinds of other things has put a fear in my heart and as I grew up in Canada, I seemed to not relate with the Jamaican people or their culture.

I feel so ashamed to speak about my birth land this way because I now know that there is an issue and it need to be fixed. I finally found the root of the problem, in order to fix our lives we must find the root of the problem and start from there. Now the healing process begin for me.

I wasn't sure the reason behind what I was experiencing. All I knew was that as I started to grow I want to be accepted by them but no matter what I did, I just could not be accepted by them because they did not see me as a Jamaican. They did not see me as a part of their community and they would never involve me in anything.

I used to love to go to a reggae dance although I never really liked reggae music but as I got older I started to enjoy a bit more of the culture, the music and a little bit more of the food. However, I realized as I tried to go out into the environment and get closer to them; that they were trying to use or abuse me. It was the craziest thing I have ever seen.

When I would not let them use and abuse me, then the hate set in. I am sure there are great people in the country, but I seem to a have a hell of time meeting any. Nevertheless, I am hoping and praying that I can meet a few like my grandmother Violet Amelia Merrick who I love so dearly.

Somehow I make the Jamaican people hate me. I wish I knew what I was doing wrong and why they don't accept me as a Jamaican. There is something about me that they don't like so whenever I would go into the premises of a Jamaican, I would carry a nervous feeling. It was as if God at left me at the door.

When I entered a place where there was Caribbean or Jamaican people -this is a real thing- people say that the nervousness I carry is absolutely insane. I would kick it off and try to ignore it but it's been happening for years.

I ignored it but as I started to write this book, meditate and go back in time; I realized that I have always had a fear of Jamaicans. I was never accepted by Jamaicans and now that I understand it, I feel like it's time not to speak anything negative about Jamaicans because I am a born Jamaican and to speak negative about them is to speak negative about myself.

Therefore, I tried to find the best thought that I could about the people. The country is a beautiful place but the behavior of the people shows a slave mentality, and because I was not raised under it, I can't think like that. I believe that every individual deserves an opportunity and a chance to be great and that they have those things inside of them to be great and magnificent.

I did not like the idea that the poverty is real. When a family is poor in that country, for some reason it doesn't seem like there's a place or a people that will help the community. It breaks my heart and it's too much to handle. There's a lot of things about the culture that breaks my heart and hurt me and I didn't realize how much it hurt me.

When I speak about my own culture and people I speak very badly because I am so angry with their behavior and lifestyle. Since I have come to this realization, I choose to do better and be the change I want to see in my culture. I choose to be the difference meaning that I choose not to speak negative of my culture, I choose to find the positive in each person, and in myself. This is great growth in me, huge growth for me to a find this place in myself since I grew up with a great amount of fear of Jamaica.

I know my "nanny," (my grandmother) was one of the most humble women, while my grandfather was a very mean man from what I remember of him. As I got older, I realized that my nanny was an angel because she took care of over twenty four grandkids while we all slept in the same bed and house.

The house had two bed rooms and we sat and ate in the living room but most of the time we played outside. We did not do much as we were very poor and we did not have a lot of toys or belongings. My granny sold food at the market from Thursday to Sunday and came home Sunday night.

I don't remember having a birthday party as a young child. I never had real dolls, I use to make dolls out of the skin of the fruit. This was normal to me and I didn't think I was missing on out on anything.

I am the eldest of nine siblings; six sisters and two brothers but at the time in Jamaica, I only had three siblings; two sisters and one brother. I was born out of wedlock and not sure who my daddy was for a very long time but I was told it was two different men.

 I remember looking for him when I was a young girl. I was given information from my auntie that he lived in the same district away from my mother's family, so went in search of him. I am not sure how I found him but I did.

It was important for me to meet him since I had plenty of questions for him. He had other children and I had more sisters, yet I was not sure if he was my father. I continued living and accepted that he was my daddy because I was longing for the father I never had. I wish that I was brought up with a father because I feel as if I would have made better choices in the men I settled down with. I never saw him or is children again.

When I decided to travel years after, my life was uncertain. My mother seemed to have met my father again but he had died of stomach cancer. Sometimes I feel bad I wish I had more time with him just to be sure he was my father, but the one time I met him he told me I was his child for certain so I keep that in my heart.

 Daddy or not, I couldn't get a straight answer. I also asked him why did he not reach out to me and he said that my mother did not want him around. He had another woman with children who became his wife, so maybe she did not want him in my life. She's like a woman with the world on her shoulder.

I know my mother has gone through quite a bit of abuse by the men in her life including her father. I also believe she might have been in love with my father Oscar Clarke. I seem to have his last name but she never talked about it. She would never tell us since she is too proud to talk about it, so she hides it with anger or buries it with hate.

Mom never had a chance to finish school or do much since she missed much of her child hood. Mom got pregnant with me at an early age and was kicked out of her parents' home at the early age of fifteen. She was abused by the fathers of her children and I believe in my heart that she could not avoid having so many children because she was forced into positions that were not suitable for her.

I believe she did the best that she could, I respect her for that. I love her to the end of the earth and back, she is my hero and deserves the very best from us because of the hurt and suffering she endured with our fathers. Most women would have cracked or gave us away but she held on to us. No child should treat their mother disrespectful in no circumstance.

I also believe that her father did not teach her how a man should treat her. She was scared of him and so was I because while growing up with him, there were times he would throw a machete at our heads. Not only this, but it took several months to one year before grandfather saw or held me because it was forbidden for a young lady to be having sex at such a young age. It was out of the question. However when he held me he kept me.

My mother always tried to find the best life for four of her children. She gave us the best of herself the only way she knew how and I thank her for life. My mother had my sisters and myself and then my brother, who I have always thought had mental issues.

I believe that not getting the love from his father has left a huge impact on him in a negative way, and to add punishment to injure the white woman that he had has three kids. Although she has taken them away from him he still works and supports them but she has turned their minds against him.

It is quite sad because he is a great father and it weighs heavily on his mental state. He has a huge anger problem and I remember him almost killing my kid over a parking stall. I also remember as a child we moved around a lot Jamaica.

We went to St. Elizabeth where my sister's grandparents live and while we went to visit them, they stole my sister from my mother. We then had to steal her back in the middle of night and we found a ride on the back of a pick-up truck to St Mary's where we lived with our grandmother and grandfather.

Mom was willing to make a change in her life for us and so she continued to fight for us with all the abuse she faced from the fathers of her children, and my grandfather who was a very mean man. My granny was a saint, and I am not sure how they stayed together for all those years.

My grandfather took her when she was a very young girl since her mother died giving birth and she grew up with her uncle. Not knowing how to read or write, I guess she settled and I believe back in those days women did not have much rights.

My grandpa was scary! I remember him being mean and he would throw a machete at our head. Until this day I am not sure if he was trying to kill us or scare us. As I got older, I realized that my mother picked up some of the same temperaments as her father and that my cousins were as mean as he was.

I remember he was not a nice person and one day he chopped me in my knee with a machete. He was making drops another time and I decided to take one, he was so upset at me taking it that he dipped an old time Jamaican iron into the sugar drops and stuck it on my leg. I had a third degree burns and the scar is still very visible.

I was about eight years old when my uncle tied up my baby sister in a red ant ness and poured hot honey all over her. I don't understand those kinds of cruel acts and when I asked her how she felt about him, she said she forgave him because they learnt their behaviors from their father and they did not know any better. They were a product of their environment.

This is what I think caused me to hate the place of my birth, everything about that place was toxic. I have seen more sadness than a child should see. I have seen the evil that lurks in that place. There was a woman that walked around the community yelling at the top of her voice telling people that their family member is going to die and there was always a death in the community.

After she finished screaming about it, she was always right. She scared the people in the community including me and it took a year to get her voice out of my mind because she was so right. When you heard her coming, it rang in your soul for a year with fear.

I never knew that there was a world out there where we could live because we never really travelled out of our area. Most Jamaican's only know their country since they are locked away in their little village and stay there because of money and it is hard to travel anywhere without money.

Most of us can't even swim and we are surround by water. I have not had any great memories of the place except my wonderful grandma. I was born in a very hard time and I just remember sharing one bed with almost ten to twelve cousins which was ok.

We always had food to eat and was clothed by my grandma. I don't remember walking barefoot but we had no television and no running water. All we had was a tank that the rain would full up. It was better for us anyway, I think! We would walk a mile to a friend of the family to watch TV with the two antenna and there was plenty of kids especially on Sunday.

Everyone's kids were there with a hanger and we would watch bionic woman. That was a treat for us kids or when our grandmother would tell us, Nancy stories. Those times were the thrill of my life and I quite enjoyed those stories. Miss Violet Merrick was the most amazing woman God put on this earth, when you talk about unconditional love, that was my granny and I have never loved any one like that again.

I can't even compare her to anyone. She loved each and every one of her grandchildren equally and she was so amazing. A patient, kind, gentle, woman, who sang a special song for the grandchildren which went like this: (I'm on my way to heaven 7 6 5 4 3 2 1 repeat).

She was such an amazing human being that she even took care of her husband's outside child. She breast fed the child and that child grew as if it was her blood child. The child's mother tried to destroy our grandmother's life by trying to take her husband through getting pregnant for him. However, when this did not work out, the mother didn't want the child anymore.

My grandmother dedicated her life to her grandkids and I love her so much. She was such an honest woman who would not tell a lie to anyone instead she would not answer. I truly crave her smell and her face. She loved me so much and protected each and every one of us under her wings. We didn't need to be rich when we were with her. Who knew that one day I would be taken away from her!

Since my mother wanted a better life for us, she applied for a nanny job in Canada and by the grace of God she got her visa. This is where the hardest time of my life began, my whole world turned upside down. My mother left Jamaica to go work in Canada, I figured she would just send money to take care of us before returning, but in less than three years my brother and I was uprooted from my grandmother and my sisters. I am not sure of the reason but, I would assume she only had enough money for the two of us at the time. My baby sister was left at two months old with my second oldest sister.

I feel a lot of emotion writing about this, thinking about my baby sister being left behind. I couldn't bare the pain of looking at my sweet Grandma. I just remember the look on her face as if someone broke her heart in a million pieces the pain on her face kills me, I live with it every day. My heart stopped and part of my young self-wanted it to stop if I could not be with her.

I am not really sure where I got the strength to get on the plane. It was the longest walk ever. I decided to run from the plane back to her and I held on to her skirt for my dear life. They peeled me off her and life was never the same. Part of me was taken and I often felt as if it was the only good part that was taken and it didn't come back.

I arrived in Calgary, Alberta. The two oldest had gone and I was now the oldest sister. My heart was broken, they were my responsibility, she was only two months old and my mother was gone. I felt as if I let them down and wondered if I would ever see them again. I asked my mother, "why didn't you take all of my kids at the same time," and she said when we were older she would explain.

My mother always felt like a stranger since we did not live with her for a long period of time. We were raised by our grandparents and my baby sister didn't know her mom. She did not get that maternal bond and so there was a great void and no time for love to develop. My baby sister always thought our granny was her mother.

My mother did not make up for the lost time with her baby daughter but I believe my mother loves her kids based on the love she had for the children's fathers. My mother has been hurt by men, especially the fathers of her kids and I realize that I shared the same behavior as my mother did. I had to make changes quickly because it was affecting my relationship with my children.

My mother returned for my two sister four years later and what was strange was that I did not feel the same bond with my sisters anymore. I was not sure if I had changed or if it was them but my two sisters had built a bond that seemed unbroken I could not get in. We were all different people because we were so far apart.

I remember going out to a club with my youngest sister this was after we all grew up. She was upset at how dark she was and how light we were and she said that we are getting all the attention. It was a crazy thing to hear your sister say, then she left. We were just trying to bond with her but she was always a little strange.

She had two beautiful daughters with a white man, the girls were twin but it was a very abusive relationship. She stayed however since she left my mother's home because it was toxic. She said it was worse than being abused by men raping her.

I am so saddened by all this information because I know my mother as a protector. When I spoke to my sister in confidence, she told me that the father of her twin use to beat her while she was pregnant. I asked her why would she did not tell one of us but she said it was easier to deal with the beating than getting raped.

Why would my mother see that was she a rape victim and not want to talk about it or be reminded of it? It is very hard for Jamaicans to speak about rape, they were taught to hide it. I have a good friend that I met several ago, she is like a sister and has been dealing with a rape issue.

When she was ten years old, her grandfather was raping her. No matter what she did to get her mother to listen to her, she would not and told her to stop making up lies. All she could do is deal with it the best way she knew how.

When I entered Toronto, Ontario I was in disbelief that the place was full of so many colors and races and I was shocked at how big the world was, not knowing what laid ahead for the rest of journey into Calgary, Alberta. In Calgary, my mother was married to a white Irishman. It was my brother and my first time meeting him at the Calgary international airport. I remember my mother saying, "Which one do you think is my husband? Do you know?" I said to her, "they all look alike I don't like none of them, I just want to go back to my grandma!"

It was the first time I laid my eyes on snow so it was definitely a culture shock. I wondered how anyone can live in this condition since it seemed impossible to me and I wondered how I got in such a situation as this. I was to begin school soon, at St. Michael's School. They held me back a grade because of my accent and they said I was not ready for grade 3 but at the time I really did not care because I did not want to be there anyway, this was not my home – these were not my people.

In this new place I was not sure of anything and I did not understand the culture nor was I accustomed to the rules. As I grew, I became scared of everything and everyone because everything was different and they were different and I began to learn that I was different. I worried about all the things that set me apart from the kids in my class and I developed a kind of self-hate.

I was teased about my hair, my nose and anything about me they chose to make fun of. They hated my color especially. I use to love everything about myself, I was a good little girl and had appreciation for most things around me. I appreciated life even though I never had much, but I never knew what I was "missing."

Coming to Canada changed the innocence about me. I got more than what I needed and became spoiled and unthankful. It seemed as if Canadian kids were not very thankful for the lives they had. My mother always felt guilty because she left us in Jamaica from a young age so she wanted to make it up to us. When we got here we had more than we needed and it was hard for her to give us so much but she felt the need to and my other sisters were still in Jamaica.

Growing up here in Canada, I lost a lot of the values and culture that I grew up with. One culture is too strict and the other is not, there was no balance. In school, my brother and I tried hard to adjust to the lifestyle and to fit in our school but at home with a white father, I had a hard time adjusting.

I always thought she'd marry a black man and I related my stepfather to the mean kids at school who hated my skin. I couldn't understand. I hated when my mother kissed him or showed him any kind of affection or if he touched her and I would go to my bed at night time mad as hell. I didn't understand how she could marry a white man and make him our father since he looked nothing like me, or us.

I began hurting my brother so that my mother would stay up with him and not go to sleep with her husband, not knowing that one day, that man would be a great father to me and all my siblings. My mother noticed that my brother and I were lonely and having trouble adjusting, so she decided that we needed to see people of our color and race. They then decided to move from the area we lived to an area where it was multicultural. We started a new school, but the move was hard and the kids were still mean.

We came in time for the movie *Roots* to come out, and as a result we were called all kinds of names and were the target of hate because of our skin and hair. My brother was picked on more than me because he was quiet so I became a bully. It was the only way I was going to survive in this world of theirs and protect us. We were always second no matter what so I started to fight to protect my brother and myself.

I remember when I fought a boy at school for calling my brother very bad names and spitting in his face. I beat him to a pulp and the principal wanted to suspend me and give me the strap. My mother however would not allow them to give me the strap and she took it to a different level with the school board and it was settled. We stayed in school and the boy was disciplined.

My elementary years were not good and I remember having quite a bit of learning problems and challenges with students and teachers since I was much different from the students in the school. Everyone was on drugs and it was a big thing but I was not into any of that stuff. It bored me and I was more mature. I just did not want to mess my life up with drugs or alcohol. So, at this time, I tried my best to be good and do well.

2

My Innocence

I was about 15 years old when I went to *Willco*, an American business in Canada, similar to Walmart and Safeway to pick something up for my mother. I ran inside and ran right into a six foot tall, light skin, black man. He was mixed with Jamaican and British. He looked a little older but not by much – I was still young. I pulled up my shorts so he could notice me. Even now as I write about him there is a smile on my face because I truthfully adored him.

I pretended that I was older, so he would look at me. I remember bringing home a black man and telling my mom that was who she was supposed to be with. Finally, I got his attention and once I did I was so giddy. I fell in love instantly and we exchanged numbers and I told him I was 18 years old.

Eventually, I brought him home to my mom, she saw him and said, "Do you realize that this girl is 15 years old?" and he told me that he would never touch me sexually until I was of age. We dated for four years and we were together all the time. He would sleep over at my house but he was never allowed anywhere near my bed at night.

My mom made him sleep at the foot of her bed and I use to wonder if she was trying to steal him from me, how funny. They were really close and it was nice. One day, a friend of mine brought over a girl he knew from Ottawa. He introduced us, and said this is Althea, and her boyfriend. She went right over to him and started playing in his curls. I never thought that anyone could come between me and him.

When we're young we think we'll be with the person we love forever but if there was any real example of love at first sight it would be what this girl had for my boyfriend. She decided that she would have him. Of course, I was bothered by it but I thought that since he waited to be with me and that we made plans for our lives that I had nothing to worry about. However, eventually he stopped coming around as much and he was distant.

I began hearing rumors and eventually she came to me and told me that he and she were going to get married and that this was her man now. She said that she was pregnant and that I should step back. I cried and cried and told my mom and called him begging him to tell me what happened but he said he didn't know what was going on and that he would never put me through anything like that. We talked and he convinced me it wasn't true and that night we had sex and he dropped me home.

I went to a party one day and saw the girl with his family and they were all laughing, I didn't understand why at the time and it turned out that they were married. Everything she had said was true. I was devastated and told myself I would never speak to him again – and I didn't.

One day he came to my house with their baby. I was enraged and beyond broken. I said, "If you bring this baby by me again I will kill him." I actually used the word kill, for a baby. I was so angry that this woman stole my husband and my baby. The anger caused me to do awful things. We stopped speaking and seeing each other and I started going out and acting wild. Afterwards I was lost, I got caught up in partying and being in the club. Every day I was out and my mother couldn't tell me anything. I would sneak off to Vancouver and Edmonton and leave my son with my mother. This is where I got caught up in so much trouble.

I met a man named Lincoln who was very handsome and wore expensive clothing and watches. He spoke eloquently and I wanted his attention and I got it. It was the wrong attention. I thought he wanted to take care of me and my son and make me his wife but I would've never thought he would become my nightmare. We lived in a place where we didn't see a lot of black people and I think I went overboard. So, I started to talk to him. He lived in Ottawa and said he had to go back for business and if I came with him he would fly me home. I told my mom and she said don't go. I was over 18 at this point so I decided to go.

We drove and on the way we picked up a young girl named Cheryl about 4 hours outside of Alberta in a small town. I was a little concerned but he explained that she was the daughter of his friend who needed a ride home so I was at ease. This was not the story. She was visibly upset and I pretended that I didn't know what was going on. It turned out that she believed that he was her man just as I did.

Once we got into Winnipeg, there was such a storm that seemed to develop as we crossed the border into the city. We stopped and rested a bit but he didn't want to stay because he was worried about the water from the storm. We left, took a detour and pick up another girl. I asked this time feeling uneasy, and was basically told to shut up and enjoy the ride. He scared me, he wasn't like he had been before. He never introduced the other girl and she just sat quietly in the back.

We drove further and further for days and eventually we had to stop and rest at a hotel. We got to the hotel room with two beds, the two girls were in one bed and I was in the other bed and he laid beside me. I heard one of the girls sniffling and I said to him, Cheryl's crying maybe he should go check on them something's wrong. He said, "She's a big girl, she'll be fine." I got up to talk to the girl and he got angry with me for going over there. He told me to leave her and get back in the bed.

Once we got to Ottawa he got a hotel room for the girls and told me I was going with him to meet his mother. The way she looked at me made me uncomfortable. "What are you doing with my son, young lady?" She questioned. It didn't sound right and I got scared.

"Can I borrow your phone?" I asked. He was around somewhere, listening to me speak to his mother. I called my mom and told her I arrived safe and that the drive was long but before I had a chance to hear what she said, or tell her that I was worried about being there, he came and took the phone, hung it up and said, "We need to go, you can call your mother later."

I told him that I was only straying there for a few days and then I'm going home but he said, "You are going to stay until you pay back the money you owe me for the drive, the gas, hotel and food." I was shocked and I could see the true character of this man.

"You can either work the streets, strip or do table dancing." he said. There was nothing I could do. I realized that this was his plan all along so I chose stripping. I couldn't see myself on a tiny table, where all my pieces were in front of a man's face – it wasn't natural. I can now understand why these women drank and did drugs the way they did. It was the only way to stay sane in a place like this. It was like being in hell and it was all the things that God destroyed Sodom and Gomorrah for in one place; drugs, alcohol and prostitution. You needed to be a certain kind of person. I was too young and not supposed to be there and my mind was not mature enough or strong enough to be in a place like that but the will of God removed me before the worst could happen to me.

The young girl, Cheryl and I grew close because she was young and innocent just like me so we had begun planning to run away. The other girls seemed unbothered by Lincoln's expectations – it was like they had done something to their minds. He was planning to invest in an apartment so I knew we had to leave, I had to get the little girl out of here and back to her family because she would die in a place like this.

Some of the other girls were too scared to run away. Cheryl said that she had a friend she knew in Toronto that she could call. I told her to call him and we would hide and wait in a gas station bathroom until he was able to get to us. We packed up most of our things and what we couldn't take we left in the hotel. We had been there about a month, I was supposed to be sent home a week later. I would call her off and on but he was standing right there, so I couldn't tell her what was happening. He would tell us exactly what to say and we weren't allowed to deviate from the script. He was capable of things I couldn't imagine, he had even pimped out a disabled woman in a wheelchair on top of extorting us young girls.

We sat in the bathroom for about three to four hours but it felt like days. We were anxious and scared of being caught, knowing what that would mean. We stressed that they could not be late because this was life and death. Her friend showed up and we left most of our stuff. I called the police and gave the other two girls names who were with us, unfortunately I didn't know if the names were real. I just wanted to go home, I was scared to death and exhausted. Once, we reached Toronto, I called my mom crying telling her all that had happened and she told me to stay where I was and that she was coming to get me. She asked to speak to the owner of the house telling him to keep me inside and not to let us out of her sight and then she thanked him for saving me.

She was crying on the phone with me, she said she knew something was wrong and she prayed that the call wouldn't be someone telling her that I was dead. I remember her saying she loves me for the first time that I can remember. I told her I love her too and hung up the phone and started to shake like a leaf. It was an overwhelming sense of relief. In a few hours, I would see my mom, go home and put this all behind me.

They gave us dinner, a hot bath and we both lay down crying and hugging each other. I told her everything would be ok, I kept on telling her, we would be okay - things were good now. I was not sure but I felt compelled to say that things were going to be okay. I told her to call her mother immediately because she must be worried to death. Cheryl's friend asked us if we would like to go out dancing to take things off our mind. Initially I said, "No we shouldn't, and we need to keep a low profile until my mother gets here." Cheryl said, "It's okay, let's go. Lincoln doesn't know where we are. I'm sure he thinks we are with the police."

Finally, I decided that she might be right and agreed to go out. But, going to the club was the worst idea, because birds of a feather flock together – we went exactly to the place where he would find us. One of his pimp friends saw us and called him. He was in Toronto in less than an hour. He came to the club with his friends and they were packing guns and all kind of stuff. I was standing by the bar when I saw him and his entourage of men running down the staircase of this club. He was in the back looking for us. I pissed my pants literally.

I ran to the bathroom and there was no way out. I was terrified, there were a few girls in the bathroom, and I asked them if they could help me but they told me they're not getting involved. He had a big name in the east so no one wanted to put themselves in a bad position. There was one girl in there, she said I will give you my wig and I should run for the door, I did when I got a chance to run for the door I took it I ran for my life.

He saw me and he started to chase me. I was looking for Cheryl screaming her name but his thugs already caught her. I was out the door when I felt a punch to the back of my head, I fell straight to the ground and someone kicked my face and my stomach. I was being dragged to his car but I held on to the railing for dear life, screaming for anyone to help me. No one would get involved. I think he decided I was going to die that night, but he was not taking me back to Ottawa to become a prostitute or a stripper.

I decided to fight for my life and it was as if soon as I made that decision God sent me a way out. I saw a familiar face, a man that I knew from back in Calgary. He was asking, "What is going on? I know this young girl and her family." He asked again, "What are you doing to her?" He grabbed my arm and said, "You can't do this, I won't let you do this to this young girl." He was wondering why all these people were watching me get beat by this man and he picked me up and got his friend to put me in his car.

I had four broken ribs, I was very tiny back then maybe 110 pounds. They started to get heated, the man that helped me and Lincoln. It looked like it was going to be a gun war but somehow it was settled. The man, Gill said something to him to make him leave. I saw Cheryl in the back of his car, she looked at me as if it was the end of the world and I never saw her again.

My mind runs on her from time to time, but I had no way of finding her. Cheryl wasn't her real name – Lincoln wasn't his real name. I had no real information to tell the police. I was young and I had, had enough. I just wanted to go home. It haunts me every day and I pray to God that she managed to get away.

I was saved by Gill and he asked me how I got into such a situation as this? I told him that I had made bad decisions. He took me to his house, cleaned me up and gave me some food but I could not eat because I was so worried about Cheryl. I had to go to the hospital for my broken ribs and I called my mom but she was already on the plane coming to me. The hospital staff watched me and called the police, they came but I never said anything, because Lincoln said he would come after my younger sisters if I told anyone. They also had Cheryl and I did not want them to hurt her anymore, I just wanted to go home with my mother.

When I saw mom I just held on to her for dear life. I would not let go of her because I thought I would never see her again so I held on tight. I was in so much pain and I realized that I made some bad decisions in my life and this was one of them and going further in my life I needed to be more careful. When people tell you who they are the first time, please believe them. Realize that more often than not your mothers want what's best for you and know the best way to love their children.

I appreciate her every day for coming to get me even though I believed I knew best. She stopped everything she was doing and flew to Toronto without her teeth. I did not even notice until we were on the plane and this nice looking white fellow was looking at her. I said, "Mom give him a smile" and she laughed. She looked at him with a smile and I realized she had no teeth in her mouth. She laughed and we both began to cry and laugh. This experience obviously changed me, for the better and the worse. I lost my innocence and I stopped trusting people.

Back in Calgary, I still went out and tried to live my life as I was young. One night I saw Nil while I was out, we slept together and I decided I wasn't going to let him abuse me in this manner any further. I told him, "You have to live with this decision. You chose to make a life with this woman, you have no history with her but you chose her. I don't want anything to do with you." And I decided that was the last time I would be around him.

A little over a month later I felt sick, and I had missed my period. I went to my mother and told her and she said "hmm, you get catch." Her Jamaican way of saying, I was pregnant. The other woman, we'll call her Andi, had found out that I was pregnant with her husband's baby. She got pregnant shortly after needing to make a baby to save her marriage. Around this time I started dating Raphael. I decided that her husband, we'll call him Nil deserved some grief for all they had done to me, so I made him believe the baby was someone else's. He lost his mind and this made him feel how I felt.

It was time to have the baby. I pushed it out and passed out. I woke up and looked around the hospital room but I didn't see my child. I looked up at the nurse and asked, "Where's my baby?" She said that the baby was with his dad and I told her that I did not have a father for my baby. She ran out of the room and grabbed the baby from Nil and came back in the room, crying and apologizing. I asked to have him escorted out of the hospital and told security that he wasn't the father of my baby.

Nil's sister called me asking if she could come and see the baby and I said no. I didn't want them around me. They were persistent and he was persistent – he would even sleep outside of my house. He knew it was his child but Andi insisted on making my life hell. She forced me to get a blood test when he was a week or two old. I was on welfare, so they forced me to take it and to force him to pay for support. I did it, and my son got his father's last name.

It was never the same with Nil, and I just stayed away from him. I couldn't understand how this could happen to me, but I realized this was my son teaching me how to love. Christopher was created to bring two families together – he was the product of so much love. After everything she'd done, she told my son he was a bastard and she told her kids that I was a stripper. She was mean to him at first and all he did was love her.

No matter what they said about me, or about his father and I, he never stopped wanting to love them and he did. He never stopped wanting to know them and be in their lives, he was pure of heart. She grew to love him like her own and that wasn't because of me or Nil but it was his ability to see past all the hate and hurt and just give love.

I remember his stepmother waited for him at the end of her life and I was there with her, her sons and her family. Christopher ran to the hospital, ran right past me into the room, and grabbed her hand and kissed her forehead. He said, "It's time to go, even though I don't want you to go now." And she let go. When she took her last breath he fell to the ground and I held him.

Later he told me that he felt guilty that his brothers lost their mother and his was still here. The point of me telling this part of my life, is that everything that comes into our lives are brought to us for a reason. Everything is a blessing and a curse. If you told me when I was nineteen that I would grow to love Andi and that she'd become one of my closest friends, I wouldn't come anywhere close to believing you. But because of Christopher I made an amazing friend out of her and I don't hate Nil for all that he did to me and in my heart where that darkness was supposed to be, Christopher forced light and love instead.

3

Uncertainty

My second child was with a different man. I thought I would learn and understand that having a child with a man who isn't with you or won't stay with you is not the way to bring a child into this world.

I felt as though I was following in my mother's footsteps, which is not necessarily a bad thing but she had eight kids with seven different men and it takes away stability in the home. It shows that we don't have the concept of making things better, however I believe that my mother did the best that she could and I thank her every day for it. Most of us are the product of our environment. I never wanted to have this many kids with different a man – I feel that it breaks my spirit. Every time I give a piece of myself to man and every time you have a child with a man you take a piece of him and he takes a piece of you – not knowing what piece you are taking in which can dampen the soul.

I know that my second child was born for great things because the day I gave birth to her at the Holy Cross Hospital she was on TV as the last baby to be born in that hospital. It was going to be torn day the next day. From that day, there was a sadness in her eyes, it wasn't like her brother.

I was young and concerned with partying and going out on top of working all the time and I didn't take the time to realize that there were certain things that affected her more than my other children. There was a strength to her that I didn't see in my third child.

I babied my third child more than I did my second and she saw this as me loving her sister more. I leaned more on my third child than I did my second because I believed she needed me more but I couldn't be more wrong because she was the one who needed me more.

She has the heart of an angel. I feel now that I can understand that she has had to carry so much and I was supposed to support her load and in that aspect I failed her. But she should know that I love her more than I love myself. I realized that there was so much going on as my kids were being raised, with myself and in my home. As mother's we forget or don't realize that everything we go through our children carry as well. A friend of mine told me to see a spiritual healer and I thought about it for a long time as I genuinely believed that God puts things in our life for a specific purpose.

I met my second child's father in Calgary at a nightclub or someone's house, I can't really remember. He was very good-looking and if you knew me you knew that if I wanted something I would get it. All the girls I were with, said he was so attractive and I wanted him. He came over and said hello because he saw me looking at him and it was an instant connection. Things moved very quickly and heated up just as fast and within a year we were living together.

He got more and more popular but he was unfortunately a pimp. I used to tell myself that when I was in a bad place I looked like a prostitute and that's why these kinds of men were attracted to me. It's the downside of not liking or loving yourself because that's what you attract, you think that's what you deserve and what you gravitate towards. After a year I was pregnant again and once again confused.

I debated whether I should or should not have this child. It seemed that this was not the time to bring another child into this world as my life was constantly in turmoil. However, it was decided by her father and I that we would bring her into the world because she was made out of love and we would give her the best possible life we could.

It seems like my whole life has a turning point of 'unfortunately,' because this man was more caught up in prostitution than in his family. I remember him selling a prostitute named Jackie to another pimp for $2000. That's how they did it in those days, I believe. But she was enamored with him, she would not leave his side. She went out and made money just to sell herself back to him. This was a broken woman, a woman with no love, coming out of abusive situations of sexual assault and violence. He showed her the most love that she knew. I told him that karma would come back to him for treating a woman in this manner knowing he had children – daughters and that the curse of a father would fall on his children.

This girl wanted to be loved so badly that she would have done anything for this man. I'm not sure if it was because he was a sweet talker or just handsome but women all over the world just loved him - young and old would crumble at his feet. He was making insane amounts of money and he could buy a brand new car. He was selling females to other pimps and I told him life will catch up with him.

The ladies would not leave him no matter what, they wanted to sell their body and give him the money,

I guess. Sometimes I think I was just as bad as him because I would take the money knowing where it was coming from. I opened my life to things that were not of God.

2nd child syndrome fell heavily on my first daughter. She was always envious and upset about how I treated my second daughter. She believes that I don't love her but I can assure her I could never feel anything but love for any of my children. I believed that my younger daughter was so much smaller and seemed like she wasn't strong enough and I had to be more protective over her. Although it turned out she was the stronger one. I believe and realize now that she needed more attention than her baby sister needed. She was the one strong enough to leave me, she has a heart of stone.

I would have never thought that I would be in a position like this where one of my children would abandon me. I've done a lot in my life but no matter what was happening they were first and they were never left without food, shelter or home. I made sure that they were taken care of but they did not feel loved by me, they felt that I did not protect them and I put them through too much.

I felt that they felt it a million times more but in order for me to deal with this pain of my child turning her back on me I had have a spiritual awakening. I had to fall on my hands and knees and accept the Lord and believe that He is my strength, my rock and my fortress. If she knew how hard it was to carry her for nine months, the stress of being beaten while pregnant with her and trying to protect her inside my womb. I built my faith around God and a spiritual movement and awakening and in finding different things and different ways in life.

It doesn't matter how spiritual I was, it is a matter of how strong I built my mind. I was a target and I wouldn't remove myself from the danger stains. It would lurk around the corner from me because it knew I was vulnerable and it would catch me every time but the love of God saved me every time. It taught me lessons and these lessons I could never seem to learn because they came one after the other. What I mean to say is that you may think that I was stupid because the more I got the more I would look for.

For some reason I was looking for happiness in all the wrong places. I was looking for happiness in another human, I was looking for happiness in a man, and I was looking for happiness in material possessions. I was looking for happiness in all the wrong places. Here I go again with the last terror of my life before the great awakening. I love my daughter but I have taught her how to be rude. I didn't seem to do well with her and she's very disrespectful to me but I have no one to blame but myself since I let my children into my personal life.

As mothers we must set barriers between us and our children and build a respect. I have learnt in life that respect goes a long way, sometimes it's the difference in making it in life or not. My first daughter was suicidal at a very young age and now I am wondering if I was part of the reason why she felt like that. I have to live with all those feelings for the rest of my life and most of the time I believe my girls don't like me no matter what I do for them but I continue to love them with all my heart. *Please God help my kids to know my heart.*

On Sunday December 9th 2:34, my daughter wrote to me, *"You're an incredible woman, a complicated woman - but incredible nonetheless. When you hurt I hurt as well. I am your daughter and it doesn't matter if you tell me not to cause when God-sent me to you in your tummy we were bonded spiritually. I don't expect anything from you except unlimited happiness I will never leave you alone to be sad. I love you mommy you're never alone."*

When you have a 14 year old daughter who has some serious emotional issues and is need of the love you often feel you're missing on those days when you feel like your back is against the wall and all odds are against you, look into that little girl's face if you can't find purpose or reason to fight through those dark days. We need people to love us but almost more importantly we need to love ourselves. You are immaculate and destined for greatness. Your story isn't over it's just the beginning I love you mom.

December 18th (my son's birthday), my daughter wrote, **"Why are you talking about my girlfriend. Defend your husband   all you want but I'm officially done with you. Run behind your man it's what you have always done. What I'm not doing is letting your poor judgment of character affect me anymore in my life, so don't come to me with your problems, go to your husband and stop texting me about him because I don't care about him and any woman that would not address their husband about making their daughter feel uncomfortable is a coward.**

You think you're so high-and-mighty and I am not your mother, well you made so many mistakes when it came to me I can't even count I don't need you texting me with your nonsense, bad energy and bad vibes. All I was trying to do was have you and my sister over for dinner on Christmas Eve and you have managed to make it about your husband, good luck to you and your husband. You think I'm joking you don't realize how hard I have been trying to mend a relationship we never had. Best of luck."

I know I've done things in my life that I am not a proud of and I can't continue to live from those dark places. I can only apologize for my behavior so many times. I did the best that I could do based on my situations and my circumstance. I will write in this book that, I have never loved any of my children more than the other. None of you were ever hungry, I never beat you, and you never lived outside and were never in any danger out in the cold.

I did my best and that's why all four of my children's views of our life today, help them to make choices as an adult. The choices that you make based on your adulthood is based on you, not me. Although you don't want to have anything to do with me, I still love you and I still hope for the best even though you all have chosen to take yourself out of my life in one way or another.

As for my second daughter, it's been three and a half years and I haven't seen your face, I haven't heard your voice and I haven't felt your warmth. Sometimes I forget what your voice sounds like and I forget what your face really looks like. I remember when you two girls were growing up, I went to bed for fifteen years straight without sleeping at nights. This was because I was worried that I would stop breathing, my heart would stop or I would die in my sleep and I would have to leave my children in the world by themselves. No one can love them like me, and then there would be nobody to look after them or to love you guys the way that I do.

I am broken inside from my two daughters because they have left my heart empty and hurting. There is a great void in me and it is God above that's holding me up. I wish that they had their fathers in their life and I know for sure that my eldest daughter is missing a piece because of not having her father around.

When she met him she was nine or ten and I had to send her away with my first husband because her dad was strung out on cocaine. I made a decision to keep him out of her life and I'm not sure even now if it was not one of my best decisions. I wonder if I actually I hurt her more than I did well for her. As a child she's been searching for this feeling of belonging and as a grown lady she still fights for that feeling of belonging to the point where no matter how much I tell her I love her she doesn't seem to believe it.

From all my toxic relationships with men I finally understand why my daughter is a lesbian. I believe she did not want to see another woman go through such pain as she saw me go through and I cannot help but think that I had something to do with the choices that she's made in life. Having a woman as her partner was one of the hardest thing for me to handle or understand. Growing up Jamaican, it was a taboo thing to be gay and I was never taught to accept it or tolerate it – this was the culture.

I was raised differently, but I still love her unconditionally. So I continue to love her more and more each day, just like all my children. But for some reason I can't seem to reach her. There's a competition in my marriage with her, she believes that I give my husband more than I give her. She does not understand that it's two different kinds of love I have for each of them. Sometimes I feel as if she hates me. I can't seem to get through to her and I can see that she's in a multitude of pain and that she's angry.

She's angry at her sister for leaving, for walking out on her, she's angry at her father walking out on her and now I believe she thinks that I've walked out on her. I feel like I have nothing left to give and I feel like I've given all to my children, everything that God has given me to give out. I honestly don't know if I'm capable of giving anymore but if I can find the strength to give more.... I will search as deep as I can and see what I can do.

I dedicate my love and I've dedicated my life to my children. I could have run away, I could have left and I could have done so many other things but I want you guys to realize that I held on the best way I knew how and for me not to be able to see your faces and hear your voices it seems as if I've loved and cared for you guys for no apparent reason, and that the saddest thing a mother could ever feel.

For all the children that have picked up this book throughout the world, there should be nothing in this world that stops you from seeing your mother's face. There should be nothing in this world that stops you from loving your mother, it's a great loss. The love between a mother and daughter is a gift from God and when we throw those things away it's a deadly loss.

To each and every son and daughter, just remember that there's no one like your mother and your father in this world, they are your life line. You exist because of them and God and you must honor your mother and your father. You must love them unconditionally as they love you.

For my children that will read this; to my son, my prince, my king God knows what he did when he made you first. You've never left me and you've been my back bone from the day you were born. By being my strength you have helped me with your sisters and put your life on hold. You stopped living to make life easier for them and myself and for that you are my love and I respect you and I honor you.

One wish I have before I close my eyes to die is that, I pray that the lord above will grant me one more wish and that is to see my second child

Daughter love you and there is nothing on this earth that could ever stop me from loving you. This goes for all my children, I love you now and forever with my whole heart – never forget that.

4

The Hole in the Sock

My first marriage was a disaster, nothing was right about it from the beginning to the end, it was a toxic relationship. I took wedding pictures, they were lost and I never even saw them. There was no evidence to show that we were married.

I was married to a man that was in a half-way house. I thought at one point in my life that he was my soul mate and he would do right by me but I was wrong and no one could tell me any different. He was more obsessed with me than any man that I had ever been with but it was not love, it was something crazier.

Like Nil, he was one of the most handsome men that I knew and I had never seen a man that fell in love so quickly, there was nothing he would not do for me. I remember wanting a camcorder for Christmas so I could video tape our daughter, my second daughter. He left the house and went straight to the *Brick*, he broke the recorder on the stand of the floor model and ran straight through the door.

They called the police on him and he hid the camera in the bush. The Police then caught him, they beat him and asked him for the video camera but he told them that he didn't know what they were talking about. I got a phone call at home to come and pick him up from the police station but he was not charged because they could not find a video camera. I picked him up and I asked him, "What the hell were you thinking and why would you do something as that?" and he said, "You wanted to record our daughter and I want to make sure you get everything you need." I told him, "I didn't tell you to go steal it. I assumed we would save up and buy one not for you to walk into the brick store break it off the stand and run! And how were you able to hide it?" He then said to me, "I ran and jumped a fence and I stuck it under a doghouse, I jumped over the fence before they came back over for me so they didn't bother to go back and look for it."

When I talk about him being crazy, I mean that he had no fear in his heart. He would say the strangest and the weirdest things to me and I really thought that was love and I was excited with it. You can actually see how screwed up I was that I couldn't see his issues and I couldn't tell the difference between crazy and real love. All the beatings, the boots to my face, the name calling, him being jealous and pulling out my weave in public telling me that I was looking at other men funny, was what I thought I deserved.

He was from Edmonton and I lived in Calgary and when it was time for him to go back home he would not leave my side. He became very obsessed. I remember saying that I wanted a man that was obsessed with me and I got exactly what I asked for. Words are powerful and you just might get it.

This relationship turned in to hell. I remember I came home with my friend one night, my friend of eight years. He was still with me but somewhere along the line in that eight years he found a friend called *cocaine* and after that everything changed. They say that when someone is on cocaine, the devil takes their soul. You're not thinking spiritually, you're thinking of your own wants and needs – you would sell your soul to the devil for another hit.

He became quite abusive and obsessive. He would beat me because he was paranoid and every time he was high, he would accuse me of having sex with other men including his brother. All the while he was cheating, it destroyed my self-esteem and the abuse only added to it. I remember being pregnant and falling asleep because I was so tired and sick from the pregnancy.

A friend of mine came over to visit and we talked briefly but I just couldn't keep my eyes open. She said she would go downstairs and wait while I slept to make sure I was okay. My husband came home and saw me sleeping and slapped me on my forehead. I jumped out of my sleep and he shouted, "Why would you leave your friend downstairs, while you are upstairs?" He then kicked me in my stomach because He thought I was being disrespectful. I remember thinking something was wrong and I had her bring me to the hospital. They checked me out but we didn't tell them what happened and they told me I was okay but the baby was stressed.

At six months pregnant I finally got Darren arrested. I was so overwhelmed that I forced my labor. I told the doctor I heard I could take castor oil to induce labor and he said I could but advised against it strongly. I asked him if it was safe and he said that she was big enough to survive. There was obvious dangers so I took my best friend with me to the drug store and bought the white castor oil and together, we took turns taking teaspoons of the castor oil.

She got sick and ran to the bathroom, while I vomited and got really hungry. She managed to leave the bathroom and run out to KFC and brought me some food. I ate and ate until the pain came and I told her, "I think I'm going to have a baby!" With her British accent she said, "Oh no, you're not! You cannot do that here!" She then took me to the hospital.

I remember the nurse looking at my feet and for some reason I remember clearly that my sock was torn and my big toe was sticking out. "Oh my, what holey socks you have." The nurse laughed, but I did no laugh because I was in too much pain. The baby was under distress and they needed to get her out. They inserted the monitor into me and pulled it out like a rope. My sister came to visit me and saw them removing the machine and fainted. I had one friend on the toilet and one fainted.

I was in labor for around 5 – 6 hours and gave birth to a little tiny baby about 2.3lbs. She looked like an alien. She was placed in an incubator for six months. I felt so terrible, the guilt was devastating and I could not believe I did that to my baby girl. To this day, I still cannot smell or look at castor oil.

The tests came back, and they found cocaine traces in her blood. They asked me if I had done cocaine because the traces were so high in her that maternal usage would be expected and I told them that her father was a crack head. They did not believe me so they tested me for AIDS and drugs. They were looking for a reason to take her away from me, as if her hostile birth wasn't reason enough.

They became comfortable with me after all the tests became negative. She had brachychardia which means a low heartbeat, so I slept with her in the premature baby unit until she was seven months old and then I took her home. Darren was in jail when she was born and when he came out, he wanted to see her. I know to this day I should've said no, but I let him and not too long after he was back in the house. This was my cycle of abuse, and I was afraid of him. I knew I should say no but the answer was always yes.

I caught him in hotel rooms with prostitutes, I saw him O'D and he stole my mom's car. It was a disaster and the cocaine made him fearless. I always knew when he was going to cheat because he would put his music box on his shoulder and walk out of the house and up the hill. I made a friend with a girl I defended and it turned out that she was the one he was cheating with. This is where I think most of my trust issues stem from.

I remember running away. He put the fear of himself in me. You know how you're supposed to have the fear of God, I had a fear of him. My kids saw him beating me and I feel as if I was a weak woman to allow a man to treat me like that in front of my children. He stole my son's Nintendo, his bike and he seemed to steal from the other kids but not his own child. Whenever I think about the pain I cause my kid my tummy aches because he would even steal her little money that she would receive for her birthday present but he wouldn't take her toys.

He became even more reckless and he would do anything and everything possible. He stole my vehicle and he had it for 3 months although my children had to get to school and I had to get to work. I was running my own business and I had to take the bus, walk I and do whatever I could do to get where we're going. He was in and out of jail for years, 8-9 months at a time. But this time away did not change anything,

When he came out, it was me that he wanted. He was obsessed with me and the drugs, and for whatever reason I would take him back. That was the part of me as a woman that I could not understand, why did I think I deserve the abuse and the lack of self-love? I have never forgiven, this man and I hope that through writing this book that I am able to release some of the pain and anger I've held on to for many years.

A lot of people told me that he was nothing and that I should be able to just get up and leave but when somebody is in your mind and in your heart they can put you in a position of fear and stress that makes it very hard to leave. There are a lot of women in situations like that and people need to understand that it's not that easy, when the mind is trained in fear that is where you live.

The funniest thing is that his mother made him that way. No matter what he did to us and the children she always found a way to protect him and she believed that his life was screwed up because of me. She came to me one day and told me let him use the car because he's trying to get a job and if anything happens to the car we'll take care of it. While the car was in his possession, he took my steering wheel, my stereo and everything else in it. When we found the car, the car had nothing left. Everything was gutted out of it, a brand new Honda Accord. All I could do was cry and I remember with all the problems going on, his brother went out and bought me a new car.

I remember how severe things were and I started getting breakdowns, it was intense. I started getting sweaty hands and could not focus any more so I had to find doctors to confide in. I could not look in people's face because I thought they were noticing that I was losing my mind. I had to lock myself in a room and stay away from people because at this point in my life I was in a scary dark place. I felt alone in this world and I had to take care of my children but I was too ashamed to let my friends and family in.

The doctor prescribed pills and the pills made me feel as if I did not exist on this planet. I would take these pills once a day and I would lose myself, my speech and I had no energy to speak nor energy to make any decisions. I would just take the pill and sit there and stare into space and I knew something was wrong because no kind of medication should let you lose yourself. I needed help because I was losing control. I didn't know what to do, I knew I had to go away and I needed a break but I was worried about my children. I don't know what would have happened to me if I was unable to take care of them.

My problem was getting dangerous as I began contemplating suicide or hurting myself. I was worried that I would not be able to take care of my children, so I called my friend in Toronto and I remember crying on the phone and telling her that I was lost and broken. I didn't know where to turn and I needed help. I explained to her that the doctor put me on medication but when I go on the medication I couldn't move. I was numb and it made me want to kill myself – I told her that they make me feel as if I don't exist. She said to me, "just come to Toronto, I will take care of you."

I got my mother in law to watch my children, because my own mother wasn't able to. Even though she didn't like me, I had no choice because I needed to get well. I left to go to Toronto for two weeks and I was so scared on the plane that I had a panic attack. I had to take one of the pills because it was the only way I could fly. My friend picked me up from the airport and she was looking at me like there was something different about me but I was so out of it that I couldn't even explain what was different.

I just kept on nodding to her and she knew something was definitely wrong because if anyone knew me, I'm a chatter box. She took me back to the house and asked me if I was hungry but I told her that I wanted lay down. I just wanted to take my medication because the medication was wearing off and I couldn't deal with people. I couldn't deal with the questions, I couldn't relate to anyone and I needed the pill to focus.

I took the pill and I could not feel anything. I was told that my pupils in my eyes were dilated, and they will never let me take another one of those pills I was going to have to pray and breath and eat healthier. I had to find another way because they removed the pill and I was unable to take another one. They just held me, fed me and loved me and it was enough to pull me out. They even prayed with me day and night.

I remember my friend's sister was a nurse and she came in the room and asked her what kind of pills I was taking and she told her sister not good ones and that I need to stop immediately. The ten days they took me off the pill, I shook I was shaken and I was scared to death. I thought that I wouldn't be the same again and that I would never be able to live without the pills. However, they fed me, massaged me, took care of me, talked positivity to me, told me that everything will be OK and that I'm strong enough and they give me all kind of green Bush to drink.

Within 10 days they pulled me out and when I was ready to leave Toronto I never felt so strong in my life. I felt stronger than 10 women together and I knew that I had a reason to live and the reason that I had to live was my children. When I got on that plane I decided that nothing and nobody or anything will ever put me in that position again to be away from my children, so I came back stronger than ever.

I was ready to fight whatever fight I had to fight so I am writing this book and telling this story the best I can. I want to let all the mothers and fathers out there that are going through something know that you can fight, you can end it and you can look for help, they don't have to even be a family.

Through my crisis and the things that I was going through, I don't remember one of my family members helping me. My mother didn't have the mentality or the capability to look after my kids and she wasn't capable of bringing me or helping me through what I was going through. Everybody was caught up in their own life, so I was stuck trying to figure it out by myself.

Most of the times they thought it was my fault anyway because they said I was rambunctious and I always made the wrong choices or decisions. I never really had the support that you should have from family, so I had to find it within myself and teach that to my children so that they would stick together but even then I still ended up losing one of my children for a moment. I say a moment because God is going to bring her back one day and because I pray for her soul and for her on a daily basis. I know my God is good and that my daughter will come home someday.

For the people out there that are facing these trials, hold on to your faith because the devil is a liar. There's nothing that the Almighty God cannot change and there is no circumstance bigger than him or higher than him. As I go through my journey, I learn all you have to hold on to is faith as small as a mustard seed. Hold on to it with everything, with every ounce strength that you have, because this shall pass and we will move on to a new chapter in our lives.

As I continue, I still stayed with this man and until this day I can't understand why. I must have really hated myself because I dealt with a lot of self-hate, however I kept along and I figured that he didn't think I was anything so why should I? When you put your life in man's hands, this is what happens. I believe there is not a man on the planet you can trust! You see their face but you can't see their heart, so I continued to try to raise the kids the best way I know how.

I remember coming home one day and when they opened the front door all I could smell is cocaine. If anybody has ever smelled cocaine or smoked crack or were in the presence of cocaine, they would know that it makes you dizzy immediately. The smell is very atrocious. He was smoking it with my children in the house and I tried to take them, but he would not let go of my kids.

I started to panic and tried to get out not wanting to take anything but he held on to my children, held a knife at my throat and told me to leave his children. I had to go out of the house without my children, so I called the police from a distance and had them go inside and escort me to take my kids out. The abuse was too much.

I remember a time where he tried to drown me. He put my head in a toilet bowl because he thought I was having intercourse with his brother. I was very afraid of him and would have never had those kinds of thoughts, but he kept accusing me of having sex with his brother. I was very angry so I decided that I might as well have sex with his brother. As I write, this I hope he reads it and understands how much I hated him and that I hated him so much, I wanted him to hurt the way he hurt me.

I think in many ways his brother always loved me because he took care of me and the kids and never let us go without anything we needed. Nevertheless, I needed to be away from him and his brother because I couldn't raise my kids like this. My husband's brother was a good man and nearly a year after I left, he went to prison for trafficking cocaine in the US. After that he was never the same and I believe that bad things happened to him in prison.

My daughter would ask me how her dad was and I told her how he use to burst my nose and kick me down the stairs when I was pregnant. She would laugh, then I would laugh and she would say, "I don't understand." I told her that he had a mean heart and that he was not nice. I have to wonder whether his behavior affected her negatively, I hope that I am wrong.

In less than three months, she met a man who was one of my customers at my salon and decided that she was going to move out of my house with him. She has never spoken to me again and I am not sure how she stayed away from me all those years. I call her once in a while but she does not answer. She has abandoned her entire family including her brother and sisters.

This year is 2018 and she left since 2015. And my daughter has not spoken to me because of a man. I ran into her the second year after she left at the UPS store and she looked at my face and told me this was awkward. That is the last word she has spoken to me but I still love her and I forgive her so that I can free my soul. I will continue to pray for all my kids.

5

Survival

I was in a position where I found myself alone and fearful. When I moved to Toronto I spent most of the money I saved for storage and living expenses. I did not have enough money left over to do much of anything. I tried to get welfare but I did not live in the province long enough to receive the government money or so they told me. I had to find a way to feed my children and pay my bills and I was left to do things that I thought were against my beliefs, with nothing left in me but fear and emptiness.

Somebody gave us a cot that all three kids slept on. I slept on the floor with one sheet and turned up the heat in the apartment so we would stay extra warm. My second daughter, was a bad asthmatic and because of the change of climate her asthma starting acting up.

We lived in Mississauga now, that's where I found the place and we didn't know how to get to the doctor because it was not close by. One of the ladies living in the building told me I could go and see her doctor and I agreed, not knowing her doctor was all the way in Brampton which is another city in Ontario. The move to Mississauga was interesting. I packed up all my furniture on a moving truck, picked out a name of a city in Ontario randomly and that's where we moved to.

I got my daughter dressed and took the bus which takes about 4 hours to get there and back. Where

I was going was very far, so we caught the bus and I got a few dollars to take her to the doctor because she was very sick. I was worried because we had no family in Ontario, no friends at the time and it was hours away. I didn't even realize I was going into a new city and by the time I got back it was late.

I had the neighbors watch my children at the time and I did not have a cell phone so I was unable call to check on them. I told my son not to let anyone in the apartment because they won't understand why we have nothing but he did the opposite of what I told him to do. You know kids! They were in a new environment and they just wanted to make new friends.

I barely pulled up to the apartment when the neighbor was running to the house. They were all running to me and dragging me and told me to come inside and shut the door. She had my children locked in the house and I asked what was going on. She then told me that the social service were there to take my children. When I asked her why they want to take my children, she said "I believe that your son took another little girl upstairs in the apartment and they saw that you had nothing there for your kids and she called her mother who happens to be a police officer."

Being in such a bad place in my life, I felt like I kept getting beaten down and couldn't catch a break. They thought the kids were in an abusive situation so they came to take them away. I was very scared and I remember grabbing my children, running upstairs to my apartment and locking the door. The social service people came after I got upstairs and they asked me if they could come in but I said no and told them to come back with a search warrant and then maybe we could talk.

I knew that I didn't have much time and I had to do something. They left a note under my door telling me that they were giving me two weeks to make sure the that the house had sufficient furniture and clothing for the children so I knew I only had two weeks to come up with some money to get my stuff out of storage.

I found myself on Dixie and Eglinton and there was a strip bar there. Although it was hard for me to go back to doing that since I was trying to clean up my life, I felt like I had no other choice than to start stripping again. I was alone in this big city and I was afraid that I would get involved with drugs even though myself control was pretty strong. I had no choice in a place with no family and I did not want to call them for help. I felt ashamed to ask for help and I believed that I had to do it on my own.

I was back to taking my clothes off in front of strange men, night after night. I knew how to dance well but had to learn how to table dance. It was very degrading but it was where I could make the quickest money and I needed at least $5000. In the two weeks I worked day and night until I made $10,000. I was a hustler, I knew how to make money but I just didn't know how to keep it or how to invest it.

It was a crazy place to be, I was surrounded with babies that were strung out on all kinds of pills and cocaine who would gather in the bathroom doing lines before doing their show but I tried my best to escape the drugs and anything of the sort because my kids were first. I was faced with a struggle and I had other dancers telling me I could make way more money if I prostituted my body. However, there was one thing I knew for sure and that is that my body is my temple and I could not sell my body for money.

Up until this day I have been called a hooker by most of the people who know me or have heard of me in passing, but I kept that part of me holy and have never abused my body. People who don't have any self-love, it is possible for them to turn to prostitution but that lifestyle like living in hell on earth. I don't know if anybody understands the expression "you have to bind your belly" but that's what I did. I bound it and did what I had to do because I had to make a difference for those children.

I never crossed the line. I came up with the money by stripping and I paid for my storage. I got myself a little car, had my children's rooms decorated, gave them their own bedroom suite and we were good to go. Two weeks later the social service people came by and wanted to look in my house, I let them come in this time and they apologized. I guess in some way form or shape they were just trying to protect the kids because plenty of kids face abuse at home.

They went through my house to make sure everything was in order and they were registered for school. They checked on them a few more times and stopped once they were satisfied. This was another reminder that I had to be careful with my children because I would have died without them. I had my neighbor up the street babysit them while I worked and I thanked them with my sincerest heart. To this day we've stayed friends after all these years.

I continued to strip for several years so that I could get what I needed and it helped me to open my first 350 ft² shop. The last time that I stood on a stage was when I ran into to the man that was going to be the father of my last child. Shortly after I moved back to Calgary, I met one of the city bylaw men. I can't quite remember his name but he used to come into the store and get his hair cut in the shop.

We use to sit and talk and I remember saying to him that I was exhausted and I was not spending enough time at home with my children. I told him that they were raising themselves and even though having this business was for them to be safe and provided for, it turned out that I didn't get to see them. I had been so groomed into having my own business and working for myself that I didn't know if it was possible for me to work for someone else.

His suggestion was that I take a break and get another job to see how I would feel. He told me about an answering service, *Divine 2000* that I could go into which took a minimum amount of time and I would not have to be in there. He told me that I could have other people work to answer the phone. I was intrigued and interested by the fact that I could be home with my children and have somebody I trust run the business because I thought that it was just an answer service.

After I told him I was interested, he explained to me that it was actually an escort service. At that point in my life, I had never had a problem with the law; no record or criminal charges and I was as innocent as they come. When he said 'escort,' the first thing that came to my mind was illegal but he told me that it was legal in Calgary AB, and I just have to purchase a license.

It obviously sounded intriguing and I would be able to continue to run my store. It could give me time to figure out things with my own business and set some plans but I had to wait until the lease was up, so that I could leave without being sued. I started doing research and I realized that it didn't take much to have an escort service since it was just an answering service and you could buy some Yellow Pages and attract business.

I thought I had done enough research, and learned enough about the legal aspect. I was tired and I knew that I needed to have my own business to make my own laws, rules and regulations. I called up their safety guide inspector and I asked him again about the information on escort services and I asked him to find me some paper from the city and print it off so I know the rules. I found all the rules, the regulations, spent $7500.00 to get the business license and another $300.00 to have an entertainment license, as well.

The city bylaw and the provincial government tell you all the things you need and I was also fingerprinted to make sure I did not have a criminal record, otherwise I could not purchase the license. Not knowing that I was being set up and used as an example, I was fingerprinted and in less than a year I opened an escort service. I bought yellow page ads, ran eight phones lines and had thirty four girls that would come and go.

I could not understand their mindset doing this job. No matter what you would tell them for the 1st time in my life I found women that were more lost than

I could ever be. Even though their mothers were doctors and lawyers, they enjoyed being escorts. I even had women who told me that this was the best job in life because they can get treated like queens and princesses and still have sex and enjoy themselves.

No matter what I would tell them about it being illegal to have sex for the purpose of money, they just wanted what they wanted and they fed off the money. There was nothing more important to them than money or their drug problem. They would do anything to get the money and it got out of hand.

It was a world of turmoil. I had escorts who had herpes that still had boyfriends and continued seeing John's. It's not easy to explain. Some of these females were so lost that they would not protect themselves from disease, in fact, they would have sex without protection. I would find myself babysitting their children as they went on calls and I would find myself answering phones just to help them.

At times, they would come in with stories of how they had no food and I even had people that were on drugs. I opened the business to break away from the stress and long hours so that I could spend more time at home with my children but instead I found myself in a worse predicament than when I was stripping. I even had to have police clearance to make sure that I was not a *street walker* (term for prostitute) or criminal.

They decided to do a sweep on all the escort services and came out calling it organized crime in less than one year. Registering that type of business was a trap so that they could come back and try to arrest you and, give you a charge and change your life. At this point I believed with all my heart that the police and government were the devil.

I remember it was the early morning, I am not sure of the exact moment, and one of the girls was at the office in a high rise building, with just phones and coaches. I was sitting at my mom's house and I got a phone call from the girl and she was a wreck. She said, "Oh my God, police came to the office with the SWAT team, they took the computer and the books! They took everything and they locked us out, they told me to tell you: don't get it twisted no matter what they're coming for you." I literally thought it was a joke, I said "you guys are silly", but to my surprise it was not a joke.

This was the most devastating thing that would ever happen in my life. I thought it was a joke and I called down to the city police and said, "I think you guys mixed up my name. I am Althea Clarke and I own an escort service called Divine 2000 Ltd. and I pay my taxes. I've only been open for a year and I paid the $7500.00." However, I was told that I had been charged for living off the avails of prostitution and for common body house.

I didn't have a house, I didn't have anybody else, and all I had was a small office that is 300 ft² so I definitely didn't know what they were talking about. I was sure it was a mistake since I was a licensed business by the city of Calgary police unit's squad team. I was fingerprinted by the police when I started so this had to be a mistake because every person that works in my business had to be licensed by the City of Calgary, so I was extremely confused.

They asked me to leave my name and number and said that they would have the sergeant give me a call back. I said okay and I sat at my mother's home, still thinking that it was a joke, it didn't resonate with me. I wasn't upset and I wasn't even scared. I got on the phone with the sergeant from the vice squad unit and he told me that he was going to take me down because he believed that I was complicit in organized crime.

The tone of his voice sounded like he had known me all his life and that he had some kind of vendetta against me. Again, I thought he was joking and told him that I don't know what he was talking about and that I thought he had the wrong person. He said, "No Miss Clarke". He gave me my birthday, my description, my office in the city and nearly everything. I realized then that I was actually in trouble.

I don't think there was anything worse than this, so I called a lawyer, told the lawyer what I was told on the phone by the police officer or the investigator on the case or whatever you may call him and I told him that they wanted to charge me. I then found out that it really was a common body house and living off the avails of prostitution charge and I was devastated. They thought I was a pimp but I was their babysitter - they all had to fill a request form before they went on any call, every single woman.

I was in Canada for most of my life and now I was looking at 10 years in prison. This was an indictment charge and I was also looking at deportation as well, back to a place I no longer recognized. My whole world turned upside down and it was as if somebody had used some kind of bad magic or something. It felt as though I woke up in in another life. I called the lawyer and the lawyer told me to come in right away.

I went to sit down with him immediately and he asked about the nature of the service. I told him that I had an escort service and I have a license from the city. I also told him that I paid $7500 and that I gave them my books every so often. He checked out the office to make sure there was nothing strange going on and he told me that I had about 10 charges, then he explained everything to me.

He called the bank and checked out the charges and told me that it was serious. I got very scared because I was a mother of 4 children. I remembered Martha Stewart went to jail and she was a superstar, so what would stop them from putting me in jail. I was just a simple black woman that thought I would try something to make a little more money to take care of my kids.

They held me for nine to ten hours in a holding cell and released me because I did not have any prior records. By this time, my family, my friends and everybody in-between had already seen my face on TV as a madam or a pimp. I didn't know what to do and I didn't know where to turn, so I prayed. I prayed as strong as I knew how. I didn't even know if I had faith but I still prayed because I couldn't face it alone.

My family never saw anything like this situation and some of them were upset with me. I was never involved in anything like this before and did not understand how I got there. As the trial proceeded I was cleaned out of every dollar I had saved because it went to pay the lawyer. The trial went on for about three years and at the end I was broke and had lost everything.

I had to get a low income home through Calgary housing with my children since I had nothing. I had lost all of my business because I gave everything up just to have this one. Eventually I had to go on welfare but having them support me was hard especially with a charge like that. No one wanted to give me a job, the only one I could get was at a warehouse and as soon as they did a criminal background check I was let go. It all came down to the city official giving me the wrong information and telling me it was legal; it was his word against mine.

This was one of the most difficult times of my life and I wanted to kill myself. I could not leave my babies and I did not want anyone to hurt them. I had to live to fight the system that took away my life and I fought with every inch of strength I had left. Finally I had no more money left to pay a lawyer or anybody else so I took a plea bargain. I had no more energy to fight the system; this is what they wanted -to bleed me dry- and I took it because I felt my back was against the wall.

I had to think very long and hard about the deal that was given. I went to court and I thought that if I was going to prison for 10 years, all I wanted to do was to see my children for the last time. I remember waking up the morning, got all three of my children dressed- I didn't have my 4th child as of yet- and I put them into the vehicle with me. I had one friend that came with me, out of everyone I knew in the world, I had one person at my side. My children and I walked into court and I left everything in in the hands of God.

I remember my son was sitting there looking at me while I was standing up in front of the court and I could see the devastation in my kids' faces. The baby didn't know what was going on, she was just looking at her mama and my son carried the whole load. I sat down in the courtroom and I looked around.

One of the girls that use to work in the agency came to testify against me, one black woman, the Jamaican black woman that worked in the office was the one who came to sit in court to testify against me, to bury me. Out of all the girls at the agency the only one that came to turn their back on me was a black woman. I carried that event and it dictated my beliefs about black women.

Sometimes it only takes one bad experience. After this I disliked their behavior and concluded that they are not loyal. I thought that way for a long time but that is not a good thing, it hurts us not them so I had to learn just to forgive and release. She got up on the stand and they asked her: "Do you know this lady?" she said yes. They continued, "Can you state this lady's name?" "Of course "she said. "Did you work for her at a Divine 2000 Escort Service? "Yes" she answered. "Did she send you out on calls to see clients to have sex for the purpose of money?" and she replied, "Yes, she did."

I realized that her testimony would sink me for 10 years in prison, away from my kids. I was asked, to take a plea bargain and I looked at my lawyer and told him that I'd rather have a criminal charge than to live my life in prison and not get to see my children grow. We took a recess and I went to find out what kind of plea I would receive.

My son's nose started to gush blood all over the court room because of the stress and they had to get a nurse to come into the court room and cauterize his nose. The pain that I saw my son go through was more than I could bare, it's a pain in my head and I had to keep telling myself that *this shall pass.* There's nothing else I could say to myself. I had to go through because I couldn't go around it, I had to take it as it came.

We stood there in the front before they read the charge and they asked me if I was going to take a plea. I told him that I was overwhelmed and confused and that I need to hear the plea again. They repeated it to me. The prosecutor said that I would get a record and no jail time, a $7500 fine and no probation. In my head, all I wanted to do was go home and hold my babies so I said I'll take it. What else could I do?

I felt that they did everything to break me. I had to pay a lawyer for three years and in the end it didn't even seem like they really cared about the crime I committed. I felt weak but I was still standing in the court room. I didn't know if I was going to walk home or drive home with my children but I decided that I was going to make them dinner and crawl into bed with them. I found the positives out of this seemingly completely negative situation. They gave me time to pay the $7500 to the court, I didn't have to go to jail and my kids were happy and healthy.

Another chapter of my life closed and I felt like maybe now I could handle anything that was thrown my way. I know these things are tests and they were there to test my strength, test my faith and teach me that patience and virtue. It also taught me to look at people and know that just because you can see their face, doesn't mean you can see inside their hearts. However, for some reason, I didn't learn as quickly as I should and many more lessons were coming my way.

6

The Devil Walks in a Man's Shoes

One of my circuits when I was stripping in Winnipeg is where I ran into Mr. B. I noticed him sitting in pervert row- that was what they called the first row-and I remember he was looking straight at me. I am not sure if he was looking in my face or between my legs but I was shocked to see him there since the last time I saw him was in Calgary, Alberta when I use to slave him. He use to send me to buy me lunch and do the errands.

I finish dancing on stage, got to dressed and sat down beside him to talk with. Since I knew him quite well, he asked me what I was doing out here and I told him that this is work for me. I asked him what he was doing out there just for small talk and he told me that he was stripping in the downstairs area of the building. I felt uncomfortable looking at him because I was just naked on stage but he invited me for dinner I said yes.

I was very lonely and home sick. I missed my kids and a friendly face was what I needed. It was my last week there and it was time for me to move to the next job. He offered me a night at his place and I was grateful to stay there until the morning because I was in need of some good cooked food and some company.

As I left the strip bar, a man with a Bible looked at me and I remember him saying to me that I didn't belong there. My words to him were, "where do I belong, who's going to pay the bills, who's going to take care of me and my children and who's going to take us out of the rut we are in."

I was tired of hearing what I should or shouldn't do but his voice resonated with me and I could hear it in the back of my mind from time to time. No matter where I went to dance on stage, his voice was in the back of my mind. I figured it was time to get out of this lifestyle because I am was not getting any younger and my children were getting older and starting to understand everything.

I realized that Mr. B was going through some stuff but I already had my own problems and did not want to take up no one else's. I saw that he was not in a good place in his life because he has five kids and all of them were from different women. He had been in and out of jail and had a football scholarship but I believe he lost it because of selling cocaine and other charges. He was busted, got multiple records and he could not go and play in the USA. I think he felt lost after all of that trouble in his life

I believe after this took place is when I ran into him. He was living with a woman and I am not sure of what their story is or was but I got to realize that she meant a great deal to him. He just did not seem to get it together. I was lonely, he was a very attractive man and we were both adults. From that one night, things got heated and we both started thinking about each other.

I would call him on a regular basis until he disappeared to another woman house. He was the ladies' man, and sooner or later he would come back. I became pregnant with his kid the night at his home we got sexual and I guess I should have seen this coming.

He seemed to have more problems than I could handle but sometimes your heart wants what your heart wants. Who would believe that at the age I was I was able to have more babies and I was shocked. How it possible was for me to get pregnant at thirty-eight years old but I guess anything is possible and when God has a plan for you, he delivers.

***On the next stage I performed on, I remember climbing the stripper pole, spinning and feeling very dizzy. I was about to lose my grip but I tried my hardest to hold on and then I came down slowly. I felt like I wanted to throw up and I didn't have any idea what was going on. One of the girls that was working with me at the strip club mentioned to me that I should go and take a pregnancy test and I laughed at her and said that I was getting over the hill and to me my eggs were too old for me to be pregnant but she told me that anything is possible.

I stopped off at the drugstore and bought a pregnancy test. My fellow workers and I stayed in the same house when we are stripping and we looked out for each other so we became family. I decided to take the pregnancy test and since we were all tired, we left the test in the sink in the bathroom and went to sleep and when we woke up in the morning the test was positive.

One of the girls ran back to the store to grab another couple of tests because we thought we left the test too long and it did not work but we retested it and it was accurate. I was somewhat stressed but that little blessing was going to change my life. No more smoking cigarettes and no more stripping. This was going to stop me from ever putting my foot back on a stage and I have never putting a cigarette in my mouth again.

I knew I had to tell MR B about the pregnancy but I was not sure how he would take it. I was thinking that I couldn't have a child this late in my life and I call him on the phone and told him the news. He laughed for about an hour on the phone and it seemed like he was proud and that he did the greatest thing in life. It seemed as though it was quite funny or it was a great accomplishment but I was devastated because my life was changing and I had to go back to looking after a young baby.

Confused I decided to call my son because he always has the right answer about things and he is a very honest person. My son told me that it was a blessing and that I needed to embrace it because it was a new chapter opening up in my life. Mr. B said, "I shall stand by your side and no matter what I'll be there for you." Although he made me feel better and his words reassured me a little, sometimes words are cheap.

I trust people too quickly. People say a lot of things that they don't mean, and he didn't mean any of what he said. As we continue in this journey, I decided to leave the stage since that was no place for a mother and her child. I packed up my stuff, did my last week and came home. I've never seen the stage again. Things in Mr. B's life were going down the hill and he decided to reach out to me and my kid but he manipulated me from the beginning to the end. I was now carrying his child and had no income to support me and my children.

I had to run to welfare since I had no choice. I was 38 with gestational diabetes and he forgot all about me and the baby in my tummy. We struggled and were not sure of where he was, but he found us when it was beneficial for him. I remember at one time only having 70.00 dollars to my name and he was in jail and needed money. No one would send him anything and he needed to buy medications since his blood pressure was high, so I split the seventy dollars in two, sent him half and used the balance to buy groceries for the next month.

I am sure he didn't know that, but he does not respect anything that we did for him up until this day. He racked up my credit card which I used it to wash him off (as he called it), and then there was nothing left for him in Winnipeg. He said that he burnt all the bridges he had to come back to Alberta with us to start a family which was not true, in fact he had other plans for us.

He would walk around the city telling people that he bought me a house and car, when really he came from Winnipeg with seven dollars in his pocket. He never worked but instead would dress up in a suit and tie every day to sit at the barber shop. He was clown and I don't know why it took me so long to see it. He went into a business deal with me and was to match my money for a salon but he never came up with a dollar, yet he wanted half of my business and walked away leaving me seventy dollars in debt.

He would have sex in my place of business with all types of women and he would make sex videos with other women giving him oral sex. I found these things on his camera and phone and he would hide all that filth in his car. I would have a dream or a feeling and it would take me right to is dirt. One day I had an issue and we talk all night to the point where I needed to be held, but he refuse. However I had my way. We were both strippers so you know what happened in that room, I never kiss and tell.

I was just passing through and after this wonderful night, it was time to travel to my next destination. I had no intention of seeing him on that level again. Like I said, people come to teach you lesson and it was a very hard lesson that I learnt. I am still getting over it.

I was 38 years old when I got pregnant with daughter from that one nightstand of stripper fest. He came to break me, destroy me and take everything I had, he almost took my mind. This was one of the worst moments in my life. I thought that this was my Prince charming but I seemed to have turned out to be "The devil wears shoes." You could almost say, "The devil wears Prada" *(novel by Lauren Weisberger.)*

There is nothing that I wouldn't have done for this man, I have even put my children in danger for this man. Everything about him was no good and I couldn't see it because I was **blinded by love.** I really understand that statement now because I was so blinded that I was completely fooled by this man. If I didn't have my son around me, I probably would have lost my mind and my possessions because that is what this man came to take, my life and my possessions.

Fortunately he only ended up taking a jaguar, my self-respect and my self-esteem. This man was able to give me four STD's in one stride but I hold no shame to talk about all these things since I have made peace with myself and I carry no more shame. This man had no remorse at all, it did not even phase him.

I remember going to him and asking him, "what if you had given me aids? What would we do?" He told me that we would figure it out but if he never liked himself, how was he going to like me. He was molested and abused as a child and he was also given away and up until this day, I don't think this man know the meaning of being a father. I believe that he tries but I don't believe that he understands the concept.

I can't totally blame it on him, I have to blame it on the people who raised him and taught him the values he lives by. He is a great womanizer, women flock at his feet and people believe everything he says. Therefore, no matter how bad he was to you and you were to speak about it, nobody would ever believe you. I remember that one time he looked at me and told me that he is scared that he's going to turn me mad. I can't help thinking that his intention was to drive me crazy and remove my children from me.

Believe it or not, I ended up giving birth to his child. You would think that would make things better, but it took until my daughter was almost two years old before he saw her, and I was the one that had to take her to him. He has eleven children and is very proud of all of them but this also means that he has eleven baby mothers, I guess I should have seen that coming after his sixth kid which is mine.

As the story unfolds it gets worse. I came into some money and I guess I was trying to please him. I was a pleaser of men and I forgot to please myself. I really didn't know how to please myself and I purchased two jaguars, he got one and I got the other. He used his to sell cocaine to an undercover police and the car was repossessed. I knew nothing of it All he did was walk around the city and have sex with everybody that I knew and everybody that knew me.

After a while, I couldn't keep my head up, I had to keep my head down. Then it went from bad to worse. He left from selling his cocaine on the streets to put it in the freezer in my house where my daughter would find it and she in turn took it and started selling it, oh how karma works. I knew that these things were wrong and the children were trying to tell me these things but I couldn't see in front of me, all I could see was this man and I was allowing him to destroy my children.

My son started hate me (my Prince or my king) was what I called but something inside of him wouldn't allow him to leave me. He didn't leave my sight and I remember him going to my mother and telling her that "mommy needs help." He told her that all the man I was seeing wanted to do was to take everything from me but I can see it. I believe that is the reason why my third child left without speaking to me.

She felt the abuse and just didn't want to be a part of it. She didn't want to see me and she didn't want to know these things. All she wanted to see was strength in her mother. However, my son wouldn't leave, he believed that this man was trying to get rid of him so that he could destroy me and so my son hung on to me for dear life. He came with me for the ride and held on.

I remember getting the opportunity to buy a new home and the home that I had to buy was in another city not very far away. When he heard that I got the house, he told me that I should let him live in that house while I live in the old house. I don't know what was wrong with my head, automatically I should have seen that the man wanted nothing to do with me and he just wanted what I had.

Believe it or not I had bad credit and sometimes people say that all black people have bad credit. I don't know if that's true but it started to seem that way, so I asked somebody who I knew to help me out because her credit was great and she owned three houses. I became close with her and she decided to help me out but I had to do something in return for her. I asked her what she wanted and she told me that I would have to get my guy friend to be with her.

I told her it might not be possible because you can't force anyone to love you but said that I would try to hook it up. We signed the papers. I owned ninety nine point nine of the equity in the house and she owned one percent. We had the paper drawn up by a lawyer everything was done legally. Somehow he figured it out and he had a lady fall deeply in love with him. After this, my friend did not matter anymore and the next thing you know I was in court fighting over my house.

It was a long nasty fight but Mr.B was there in court with her and the minute I lost my house, he was in the barber shop laughing and tell everyone that I lost my house. I don't know how I even lost that house but as I got older, I realized that it was the will of God. I wasn't supposed to keep it. I put eighteen thousand dollars into the basement, my children and did the tiling in the house and I put another eighty thousand dollars down on the mortgage. Yet I lost it all, I gave him my power.

I remember my son saying to my mother, "that man is going to kill mom. He wants us to leave her but I will never leave until he is gone. "My son is like my protector and he feels when harm is coming to me. I noticed it more as he got older and I keep him close to at all times. To see him all grown up puts joy in my heart.

I partly blame myself. I can't totally blame him for the situation because I should have made better choices when it came to a man with kids and five different baby mothers and races. It was not only him, I was lonely. I was in a strip bar, away from my kids and trying to pay the bills. I knew that man for years when he was in Calgary and never had anything to do with him then, and now I was in a position where I was lonely and he took my loneliness for granted. I was changing, no more innocence. He is the most ruthless man I have ever met by far.

We were the only black kids in the entire neighborhood. We were in an all-white school and we had their behavior and mannerisms, so when we met a black family we were not accepted. This happened all through my life rejections) and as I got older life seemed to not change. I felt as if I had bad medicine put in me and nothing in my life seemed right. Sometimes I get flash backs of Jamaica and how I hated it. I remember how my sister was tortured by our uncle who tied her up to a tree, poured honey on her and left her for the big red ants to bite her. The place and people were evil but I had entered into a different kind of evil in Canada.

Getting back to Mr. B, He was a womanizer who he knew how to use women and how to get what he wanted. Although I kept every single record of every transaction and every mortgage payment, I still ended up losing that house in court. Do you know that sixth sense feeling you get when you know that somebody was behind it? I had that feeling that this man was behind it and I was right.

After a while we realized that he was behind it and that he talked her into fighting me for my house in court and he did everything in his power so that she would win (don't forget that I had his child at that moment). My child lost a father because even though he's around he pays her no attention.

She fights for his love and his attention and fights to belong which scares me because when a girl starts to search for their father they will use any other man to become their father. However I kept her and I strengthen her because she is my little miracle and I will talk about my little miracle in my next chapter.

It's the strength of God that pulled me out of this situation I have used my credit card to help this man out. He had told me that his life was turned upside down and I need to go get washed off (washed off meaning I think he needed to go to a voodoo woman or church woman or a blessed woman).

She charged and the money she charged came from my credit card to save this man's ass and at the end of the day this man ended up turning around and taking everything that I had he left me in over seventy thousand dollars debt with my salon, but God was so good that the debt was removed by His grace and I was left clear and free.

I continue to survive and I continue to heal and go through the blessing of Jesus Christ. The hardest thing was for me to learn to be to forgive him and even now, I pray every day for forgiveness in my heart. for again I don't know if I necessarily have forgiveness for him or I just decided that it's too hard to hate it's too heavy on my heart to continue to hate him so I decided to pray on it every single day.

I couldn't get a dollar out of him if I tried and no matter what my daughter needs she can't get it from him so I decided to take him to court and get the back payment, but sooner or later I'll get what I deserve and so shall my daughter. Most of these men think they will live forever and he is the kind of man that looks at you and laugh. He plays the devil advocate and he tries to make people believe that he is so good and kind until he burns them with his fire.

Nobody ever sees it until the heat burns them and then they realize what is happening. Until this day he still has the house but I believe he left the woman so she has been taking back some of the stuff that she bought and now he's with his young lady. This man had four babies in one year and that alone should have shown us that he values nothing but himself and thinks about nobody but himself.

He is a brat, *the devil walks in men shoes* and someday, somehow, this man will find himself and when he does, all I want him to come to do is to apologize. However, I don't think that he is there yet and he is not a big enough man. I'm not looking for anything else from him, I just I want him to apologize and know that he was wrong.

I learn sometimes the hard way. I've been abused by this man who took away my peace for many years and I thank God that I found my peace. I'm amazed at what can happen when a woman tells herself that she loves a man and she will accept anything and most men know what they're doing. They usually take yourself esteem away and move you from your friends and your environment.

That is one of the first things that let you know when a man isn't good. If he is good then he doesn't take you away from your mother, he doesn't take you way from your children, he doesn't use you nor does he try to hurt you. I believe somehow somewhere I dominated him and took away his manhood and like a lion the field or the forest a lion needs to be the ruler of is kingdom, so when you dominate a man you take away his power.

So here I was again, I fell deep in love. I don't know how many times one human being can fall in love but I don't believe any of them were in love, it was just wanting to belong and to be accepted. When you find out how to love yourself, then you will know how to have a real man treat you. As long as you know how to treat yourself and respect yourself you will not accept anything different from anyone around the world.

I did some spiritual searching, some love searching, some self-love and some hard dark truth about myself and my life. I had to start living for me and not for my kids or anybody around me. I had to eliminate almost everyone from my environment including people that I spoke to, people that I thought was close to me and people that I thought loved me. I removed myself and I kept one friend named Jesus.

I let him teach me how to love but before I got to that place I learnt that had the devil is strong and he's a liar and I built my faith in God. I had to have a spiritual movement and awakening to find different things in life and different ways in life.

My story did not come to a close, there's more that I had to encounter. It doesn't matter how spiritual I was, it was a matter of how strong I built my mind because I was a target and I wouldn't remove myself from the danger that was always around me.

Danger always came, it would lurk around the corner from me because it knew I was vulnerable and that it would catch me every time but the love of God saved me every time it caught me. It seems as if I could not learn my lesson as I faced one after the other. You would think that I was stupid because the more I got the more I would look for, and for some reason I was looking for happiness in all the wrong places.

I was looking for happiness in another human, in a man and in material possessions. I was looking for happiness in all the wrong places and here I was again. I thought that I was done having babies at that time so I was quite surprised when a couple weeks after I was feeling a little strange.

I was still on the road dancing and I decided to go and take a pregnancy test, the test was positive. I couldn't believe it I was shocked and I remember calling right away because I think it he had a right to know. I told him that I was pregnant I don't and he just laughed. I asked him what we should do and what role he was going to play because we were in a relationship.

He said he'd try to be there the best way he could and I remember asking him if we should have the baby. His reply was that he didn't believe in those things that he would be there for the child. He said that he could not give me the permission to get rid of the child. I respected his and decided to have my child right away.

I finished my circuit and decided that it was time to go home. No more dancing for me and I had to go to the doctor and check myself to make sure that I was ok. When I got home there was no more dancing, I was a mum again trying to do the right things. I got myself a little job and save the money that I had put away to live on

Things got a little tight because after paying rent for nine months out of your pocket at two thousand dollars things get hard. When I reached out to him for some help he was in jail so he couldn't help anybody, not even himself. I gave birth on September 17th, they planned a date because I was diabetic. I'm such a persistent person that I said that he had to see his child so I took pictures, called the jail and I had them go upstairs and tell him that he had a baby girl.

After this, I sat down, wrote Letters and sent pictures so that even though he was in jail, he would know what child is looked like. I even had my son forge his signature on the birth certificate. Today we have a beautiful girl but when he finally got out of jail, nobody knew that he was out. He never tried to contact us and he never tried to find out how she was.

When I did find him, I asked Him if he did not want to see his baby, he explained all sorts of stories about people trying to kill him among other things.

Being the good mother that I am I decided to bring the child to him and we got together we flew to Winnipeg. I did not have much money on my credit card, but the little that I had paid for him to see a healer.

I got my card, took the money and went to see the lady and she told him what to do. He was supposed to pay the money back on the credit card but I never saw a cent. He moved to calamari and his life was full of poorly told lies. He never told the truth about anything and people believed that everything he had was his.

All he did was did was cheat. It's unbelievable that a man could be as evil as he is. He had no respect for sex nor any woman and he doesn't respect women because his mother gave him away. He caught me and there was something about him that held me and I wouldn't remove myself from me no matter what he did to me. Now this man wanted my son out of the house but my son never left my side because this guy was worse than the devil. This man had two concerts, one in Winnipeg and the other in Calgary, he robbed the people Winnipeg and I came back to Calgary and robbed the people in Calgary and because he left me in charge of everything at the front, everything came down on me.

At the end of the day we all went down to the hotel to straighten things out and he was locked in the room with his prostitute. I didn't know any of this until maybe months after when my son said that while I was sleeping, he got out of the bed and went next door with the girl. My son said that he couldn't tell me, all he could do is look in my eyes and ask me if I had house key so we could go home. He said that I didn't have the house key and I was tired of doing this party. All my son could do was look at me and cry, he did not know what else to do. He didn't want to tell me to break my heart because he saw how hard I worked to help him with that party.

I know that I should have seen these things in him but for some reason or another I couldn't see anything in front of me. I know it is nobody's fault but mine and I want to say that you have to be careful when some people come into your life. Some are there for a reason or season and some come into your life to destroy you. This is what this man did, he came to take everything that I had and don't get it twisted, he took quite a bit.

I found out everything that he did and between the disease, the hooker and all the other stuff. I found out he had sex with a different crack head who was friends with my sister so she mentioned his name, how much kids I have and many other things so I ended up knowing who he was. We planned and I had the girl in the car talking nicely to him so that I could hear everything he said.

He told her that my child wasn't his baby and that she shouldn't be around people like us. At the same time, the jag that he was driving with passed by me so I ran to call in the tow truck and got the tow truck to pick up the jaguar from in front of the Barber shop and he was very embarrassed. This man came to destroy my life with a vengeance.

The funniest thing is that I hand up having his child and I couldn't look at her because my heart was very hard because of her father. It took a lot of prayers and praying for me to revamp myself and I haven't reached to the point where everything is vamped in myself but I'm now in the process.

I was at the point where I didn't like looking at her because she looked so much like him and I was going to the register place to cancel the license plate but I couldn't sleep because he had over two thousand dollars in tickets and he would not give me a dollar, he wouldn't pay for the tickets, he just wouldn't do anything.

This man came to kill me and if I thought that I went through problems, if I thought anything in my life was bad, this was the time in my life that I just thought I was at my wit's end. Even then I still kept on hoping for the best, I was hoping that he would bring his kids from all over the world and they would live in my house and they'd be there with me but I know that was crazy.

He wanted the new house that I bought in Airdrie but I took it as a joke. Somehow he found out the name of the white woman that put the house in her name and started sleeping with the lady, having sex with her and making her feel like she was God's gift. He talked her into fighting me for my house and we were in court fighting like cats and dogs. I don't know if God was showing me something but they he won the house.

7

The Aftermath

My sister was left behind when she was two months old and I can understand why the relationship between her and my mother was like vinegar and oil. They don't know each other and my sister once told me that she came from love into an abusive relationship with our mother. I once asked her if she liked our mother or loved her mother and she said no, not at all.

There was never any connection there and I also realized that I never knew what was going on in our own home. She believes that our mother is pure evil but I don't believe that my mom is evil. I believe that she is just misunderstood there are other out there that are evil.

I know she loves mom. It is impossible not to love our mother because she worked very hard for us. It was years later that our family was in a bad place when my sister told me that she was raped several times, and it seem as if my mother had put all the blame on my sister. I knew nothing about it and when I asked my mother about it, her reply was very poor. She simply said that little boy's penis was not big enough to hurt her.

I was saddened and broken to hear my mother speak like that about her own child, there is obliviously a great issue between them and I hope that they will realize that life is short and we are on borrowed time and I pray that they change things soon.

My sister has been going through hell and she felt like no one was there for her. That had been going on from the time she was fourteen and I was not there for her. I was the oldest so I would leave from time to time but when I decided to sit down and talk to my sister my heart was broken for her and my heart was broken for my mother, to know she could be so hateful with one of her child.

My sister also told me that she tried to kill herself. These things were so crazy for me hear from her and I sometimes feel as if my mother had plenty of abuse in her life and quite a bit of heart break as well. I don't blame her, I just wish she could find some love in her heart for her daughter. I know that my mom means well and that she loves her grandkids very much but with her own kids she picked favorites as well as her grandchildren.

Caribbean parents seem to love to hide things such as rape and mental health and it causes so much more problems. I also believe that they choose the lighter kid in some of the families. My mother did this when my half white sisters told me to get rid of my book I am writing. She was upset that one of my sisters was not happy with some of my opinions and she never even gave me a chance but this my truth.

That is how I feel about it, I could be wrong but it feels right. It was also hard for us to love and be loved and it was hard for the grandchildren as well. Out of all the children my daughter is darker and she was always left out. All of her cousins would make her feel bad because she was darker and she said they made fun of her base on how my mother was with them.

I have witnessed some unfair things growing up that has changed and hardened my heart in a huge way. I stopped loving and I am not sure if I even knew how to love in the first place. Even though I ended up in court with my cocaine addicted baby father for stealing my mother's vehicle and destroy it, I was to testify against him but just sat in court and said nothing. I did nothing but sit there.

I have seen my sibling ashamed of the situation our mother was in because she was poor and not able to help us through university. My mother could not pay for their college. I have been crippled in my mind as a young lady growing up and I lost my innocence at about sixteen years old when my step father had a break down. I think the pressure of being a father to four black kids that were not his gave him a mental break down. The pressures of the world in mix marriages can cause depression.

I woke up one morning with a feeling of fear in my heart, not knowing what that uneasy feeling was but I was sure to find out. My step father did not look himself, he seemed lost and evil or somewhat dangerous. I was not sure what it was but it was like the spirit of God was guiding me that day and I was very observant when it came to him.

My baby sister was about one year old, I picked her up but I did not want to draw any attention to her so I put the baby down. He looked a mess and I was scared. Something told me to stand by the door by that time I put the baby down and did as the voice in my head said. He looked at me and I knew that I had to get ready to run for my life.

I ask him if he was ok and he replied, "I should have gotten your mother when she was a virgin but I didn't so I will get you." I was not sure where that came from but he grabbed a big kitchen knife, pushed over the baby and came at me. I ran about six blocks with him chasing me screaming for help, then out of nowhere a police car appeared.

When they saw the white man chasing me-a young black girl with a big knife - they turned around and came at him with their guns pulled. I asked them not to shoot or hurt him because he was my step father and something was wrong with him. I pleaded with them to be gentle with him and help him because he did not even know what was going on or why he had a big knife in his hand.

All I remember him saying was that his feet was hot. They handcuffed him and put him in the cop car then I took off his sock, kissed him on his forehead and told him that everything was going to be all right. They then called my mother right away and took him to the hospital.

I feel as if there was more going on in their marriage that I was not aware of. Maybe my little sister not belonging to him had something to do with it. After all these years he is still sick and he will be like that for the rest of his natural life on medication. He has two kids with my mother but he seemed to believe that only one was his, however both of them belong to him.

Life is a strange and complicate thing. No one wants to die and we are all chasing after something. He was a good man who took good care of me and my brother and sister I will forever be indebted to him for the great life and opportunity he has given us.

I had an encounter with a friend a magnificent girl who was from Medicine Hat, She had very tiny red hair and large breasts and she was a very pretty girl. Somewhere along the line I met her through a friend and they are good people. They both grew up in Medicine Hat and we became great friends. My friend decide to move to Calgary with me where I had a small duplex with an extra bedroom and I visited her mother and Father in Medicine Hat who owned a small bible store.

The Bible store was great, she had a great up brining and she was a wonderful girl from a great family. She told me that she loved black people because she wasn't brought up around them and she had not seen a black person until they started to play football in her small town. She was fascinated by them and so fascinated by us, that she wanted babies from a black man and she wanted to marry a black man so her babies will be black.

However, she liked the bad ones, not the good ones and I remember telling her to be careful around these people because they can be tricky. It's funny how life is because she had to choose the worst one in the pack. She was so taken by him that no matter what we would tell her, she would not listen to any of us; not even her family.

I was starting to worry about her, she moved in with me but stopped coming home at night. I would always have to call to check up on her and ask her to call us. Every day we would talk about her safety. She met one man that told her that he was a player and she understand the concept of the word. She thought that he was a sport's player but when he told her he was a player he was trying to tell her that he plays women, prostitutes them and live off of them like scum.

She was from a little town and did not understand the way they talked, it seemed as if my life was set out to be around pimps or that was the time I lived in. It looked as if people had nothing better to do. I hear people say that the world is getting very bad but the world is beautiful. It is people that are getting worse!

They were always bad and in the life that I have live I have met some shitty people. This big bad world has a big bad Wolf in it. We finally moved in together and I think my son was about three years old. We became great friends and she got more and more into this man. No matter what we said or what we did she decided that he was the man and we could not change her mind.

She would have to find out the hard way and I was hoping that it would not be this hard. We could not seem to remove her from him no matter what we did and if she said she wasn't going to see him today by tomorrow she would see him. It was like he had her possessed and I remember that sometimes she would come home with bruises.

She was scared to death scared of him and I don't know if that's the reason why she wouldn't leave. I know for a fact that sometimes fear cripples you, so no matter what we said to her we couldn't get her away from him. I remember that she went and spent a night with him and she came home terrified of the dream she had in his bed, she crawled into my bed and she was in tears.

She was shaking and I asked her what was going on. She told me that she I had to go home because something was seriously wrong. She said that she had the worst dream of her life where the man she was dating was the devil and he was here to get her. It was so real that she had to leave his house immediately because she felt as if I did not leave, she would have died in his bed. She wanted to go back home the same night but I told her not to drive at night instead she should wait until in the morning.

I wish that she had left that same night because she might still be alive today. I've been living for many years and it still feels like something is missing. I feel like a critical part of my life is missing and that I am drowning in fear. I became scared of everything around me and I trust no one and I think this is the worst way to living your life. I feel like there's no purpose to my life and I continue to go through changes, situation and fears. I became helpless.

I didn't know the meaning of thankfulness or worthy, I was caught in a very hard or difficult place and I felt like every year that goes by held a different tragedy, a bigger one. The second my friend told me about the dream I said to her, "you have to protect yourself. I think it's time that you go because you are a little bit further in than you think." She agreed with me and decided that she was going to move back to medicine. She called her father and mother, left her bed and her weight set, packed up her car with all her clothes and was on her way to medicine.

To my surprise, a day went by and her parents called me to ask me if she left the time that she said she was going to leave and I said yes. She should have been there already. I thought to myself maybe she stopped off at another friend so I called the fiend and asked her if she heard from her but she said no. I then told her that she didn't make it home because her parents called and they were still waiting for her, so we were all waiting and looking for this girl but nobody knew where she was.

I had a bad feeling inside my heart, especially after the dream she had and I felt that something wrong was going on. We started to brainstorm and we began to think that instead of her going to Medicine, she took a turn to Edmonton. The dream she had was the right dream, it was a warning for her. I remember a couple of weeks before that we went to the stampede and on the stampede ground there was a lady that read our palms and when walked into the room, the lady told her that she was in danger and she was around somebody that is very dangerous.

She had to get away from him but she had to do it slowly and I said to her, "you know, between the dreams and what this lady told us, I feel like you need to do something and get home." This was a warning and the lady also told me to be careful around black men because their intention was not good for me because they are trying to put me on the street.

She scared me but after a while I stopped worrying about it, I should have paid more attention to her. She gave us protection but we were spooked so we threw it away. I've had so many things in my life that showed me the right way and still end up on the wrong path.

It was about two weeks later and nobody had not seen her, neither did her parents hear from her. A couple of weeks later, the police came to my mothers' house looking for me to ask questions and I was shaken. I knew something was wrong and it was terrible because when I get that feeling in my stomach, it is never good. They wanted to ask me a couple of questions to make sure that this was not connected to me because I was the last person to see her alive.

I was devastated and before the cop spoke I could feel my heart dropping out of my mouth. I knew that somehow she took a turn and couldn't get away from him and she end up in trouble. When they showed me the picture of her I fell to my knees- I will never forget it- I dropped on my hands and my face because I could see her little tiny body which was strangled by his big hands.

We were not completely sure who it was but in my heart, mind and soul, I knew it was that man. I felt it was that man with all of my being. I started to cry and dropped to the ground. I felt so ashamed, I felt that all of this was my fault because she came to live with me she came and met these people. However, she had met this man before she even knew me and likely that's the reason why she came up but I was never aware.

A couple of month's down-the-line the investigation began and they asked me a few questions and I answered as much as possible. I was devastated and could not even go to the funeral because I was too ashamed to look in her mom and dad's face. I just didn't go to the funeral and I found a way to forget that it happened. As I sit here and write about it, I can still feel the same ache and pain but I thank God that she didn't die in vain because they found the killer which was that same man that I was talking about.

He took her life because she wanted to go home and who knows why? We have never found out the reason why she died and later in the year he was murdered by someone, no one found his killer. His murder took place after he was released from jail and I often wonder what it would have been like if she was still around.

My life seemed to attract the most painful things but I control my life so why do I fall in situations like this? I was told that we as humans attract either good or bad energy into our life and sooner or later life has to get better. I had to start making better choices, things could not stay the same and I had to start growing, but when was the question. Something had to change one way or another.

I felt broken inside because it seemed like I was put on earth to suffer and sometimes it seemed as if there were no choices left for me. The thought of taking my life crossed my mind but then I remembered my grandmother told that us that if any person takes their life they will not see God's face and I could not bear that thought. I did not have strong enough faith in God and my situations clouded my judgment.

My mind was not strong from all the abuse, the hurt and the pain and I don't understand why a young woman would encounter such terrible situations. I needed to pray but I didn't have any beliefs nor hope, I just lived by the reality I saw. I believed in everything and anything and I didn't draw a line, I just continued to live and moved from one situation to a worse situation.

I am a mother now and I have my children to consider so the choice is up to me to change because I am living for them and not for myself. I have to find a way to change my life but how could I go about it what could I do? I searched and I searched, yet I seemed to come up with no answer. Every day I still feel empty and believe that I not worthy and I tried to control everything by myself but after a while you run out of control.

You can't control everything. God gives you a point in your life when you run out of answers and you have to seek him to find the answer. I haven't fully accepted this yet because I still believe that I control everything sometimes. At times I feel I think that I'm immortal but inside I'm overwhelmed, wounded and my spirit is broken. My heart is broken in my mind this broken and I'm wondering if it is possible for me to walk again, if it possible for me to feel again and if it is possible for me to make the best choice for myself.

Can I ever love and what does love mean? Love seemed to be sex to me because every time a man says he loved me he had sex with me but then got pregnant and he left me. I have always confused sex with love and as my journey continued it didn't get better.

At this point in my life and as I'm writing, I'm aware things will change down-the-line but at that point in my life things had gone from bad to worse. It's like those are the things that I attract in my life. Maybe, I was scared to be loved and I believed I deserved to be treated this way because I felt that people attract things that they want in their life.

Maybe I'm attracting negative things and energy in my life and I thought that possibly a psychiatrist could help me through my hardship and help me to make better choices in life. I felt that a new body and a new mind could help me be more focused and make better choices.

Sometimes I can't understand myself so I continue to laugh and smile everything off, but inside of me is burning. I cry every night when I go to bed my pillow is soaking wet from tears and sweat. I had no one to talk to and felt that no one understands the pain of a woman scorned.

I have the children to look after so I wake up every day and I pretend nothing is going on. I cook, feed them, kiss them and love them the best way I know how to love them but as soon as they would leave for school I thought I was going to die. I realize that you teach your children these things, because your children are a product of the environment you raise them in.

They sit and watch the punishment you go through and they think that's the way life is supposed to be. Their life then becomes a disaster and they try and they fight hard but they only know what they see. I showed a lot of pain and I paid for it in the long run but I feel like I've grown up at least a little bit over the last couple of years and I want to live without the pain and without all the suffering.

8

The Journey

Well it's been quite the journey. I'm now in a place where I'm searching for peace and it is very important for me to find. I am lost, struggling to breath but I'm putting God first and I'm working really hard at strengthening my spirituality, my emotions and my thoughts but as I study and pray I find it gets hard, since there is so much blocking my path.

To be spiritual and stay committed to the journey I learned that I must be patient with myself and leave room for growth. I must not to be so hard on myself because we all make mistakes from time to time and correcting them is the right approach. I need peaceful thoughts and my thoughts a lot of the time are negative.

When I continue to think of something bad, it's like opening up a new can of worms. There is an expression which says, "The devil is a liar" and it is true, he will put the wrong thoughts in your mind and run with it. I keep saying to myself that I trust in the Lord but I don't feel my trust is strong enough. However, as the people say, *practice makes perfect*.

My anxiety, emotions, fear, stress, and thoughts all get wrapped up and when that happens I forget that God exists and I forget that he's standing by waiting to help me. I realize now that without God I could not be here still or in the position that I am because He has saved me in so many ways that I can hardly explain.

I am now learning to change my thought process and I am learning that not everything that I think of is of God. Not every thought that I get is a good thought and sometimes you have to pray on those thoughts or learn to remove them. How do I remove them? I just continue to say in my head and in my heart, "I surrender to you God." I surrender my thoughts to him I ask him to strengthen my mind and Walk with me.

I try my best not put my feet on the ground before I pray in the morning or before I give him thanks. I don't always do it but I try to do it more. I also try to meditate on his word on a daily basis to get to a higher place to be more spiritual and more at peace with myself. I realize that anger, stress and hate places a big hole in your body and is like a disease that contaminated your body and mind.

I had left a place that was healthy for a place of contamination and I'm fighting hard to heal myself. I learned to be thankful for my house and for my whole being including my organs to my eyes. I have been searching for many years, not sure what it was and sometimes I thought it was financial riches, material things and youthfulness; but no matter what I found or what I got I still had those toxic feelings.

I was walking around without peace, and how can a human live in the world without peace? Their lives will be awful because you will never find anything to be happy about if you don't have peace. I find that I'm trying to silence myself, listen more and not react to things. I let the spiritual affect everything else and what a great change it has been!

Nothing is easy about it but it is possible and for the last two years I've been holding on tight to God and positive thoughts. I believe I was always a spiritual person but I just got caught in that whirlwind trying to control everything and everyone. Now I finally realize that I can't even control myself and that was an eye opener.

My ego is one of my biggest problems because it takes over all the time. Sometimes I feel like I have a split personality (as if there was two of me running around). My ego often told me what I should do, what I want and what I need but it never felt right. It just created more and more problems and the ego gets worse to the point where I lose myself.

The ego is another force or entity from another place and I have to bury and hide it. I pushed it in the back and kept pushing it out of my mind little by little but it's hard to get rid of it totally. It wants to control your mind and it gets angry when it can't control you anymore. It makes you feel pity, sadness, guilt and many other emotions because it doesn't want to leave and it wants to control you but I choose to put God first. I chose to have God show me my footsteps and walk in front of me and beside me.

I started to see miracles and this is where my life has changed drastically. I found God, I started praying and I started talking about the things that I've been through and the pain that I've encountered. The more I talked about it, the more I cried and the more I released myself. I keep talking about the things that I was ashamed of and it would help me to know that those things were what creation my strength and molded me into a great person.

I would share them on Facebook and I would share them in everything in my everyday life. I had to get to the point where I stopped feeling the shame and guilt so I could live in the bliss, knowingness and love. I still have a little bit of shame but with time I will get over it and I was getting over it.

I would talk about God all the time, I never have a conversation on a daily basis without God. I try to never have conversations about negative stuff and I do my best to stay focused and keep my eye on the prize. I try to talk about love, wisdom and patience and I speak words that are uplifting because our words are very powerful and we can cause harm to ourselves by using the wrong words. We must use words of love to change our situations and circumstances.

Of all these things, I am filled with blessings and with things of passionate love. I listened to inspirational thoughts, strengthened myself and I learned to love myself. I began meeting people of God and I find that like-minded people stick together. I also realized that if a person in your corner is not routing for you or lifting you up you must remove them from you environment permanently.

I worked hard for God to come into my life. I can feel the change, I can see the change and I pray to the point now where I shake, I get the shakes and they call it the Holy Spirit. I talk in tongues and I realize my life's journey and the things that I had gone through was not to make me weaker but it was to make me stronger; and God has placed people and things in my life that I can reach my full potential.

I am placing these life lessons on paper to share with the world and sharing my story with people to help save them because I want them to know that their situation does not define them. You are not alone out there and the life you live today doesn't define your tomorrow. Have your faith and know that all things are possible.

I've wrote a chapter in a book called *I Am a Brilliant Woman: Volume One* that became an Amazon best seller. More than anything in the world I found true love I never understood what love was because what I've been through in my life. I confused love for sex and I confused love with other things but I now know that they have nothing to do with love. Love is patience, kindness and trust.

This love am speaking about is sensitivity and embracing God, as a matter of fact, love is the spirit of God. Every marriage union needs this to survive and should be covered by the grace of God because without it, a marriage will not survive in today's world. I know that there's a purpose and a reason for my life and my struggle being told will somehow help some people out there in the world.

Embrace your struggle because there's a reason behind it. God is going to guide you and lead you there as long as you allow Him to. There is no great man that hasn't suffered or struggled in their lives. Everybody in the world has to do their time and pay their price, but Jesus Christ has died for us, so be strong in your faith and be strong in God.

Love unconditionally and forgive every person that   has done you wrong so that you can find peace inside yourself and the riches that the Almighty God has for you. Learn to forgive because forgiveness is the key to success and giving forgiveness is the key to your soul and faith. Hold on to your faith as small as a mustard seed and leave those things in the past.

God is so good and so gracious that he covered me and is taking care of me. I found a good man and a good man is not based on money or on looks but by his character that God has given him a character that can't be bought.

I hold on to my faith, I love myself dearly and I am so thankful for being alive. I realize that my life is precious and that I am here for a reason and a purpose. I'm here to make changes in millions of people's lives and to make a difference and I now know that. I want to begin to give God thanks and praise for everything in my life, the good and the bad.

I know that I have been through a lot of heartache and pain and as I sit here today writing this book and telling this story, I cry a little because it releases the tension. I cry because it frees my soul and I cry a little because it removes the shame.

I'm not angry about anything that I've gone through and I don't hate anyone for the things that they have done to me. The reason why I'm explaining this is because I didn't give them my power and I didn't allow the people who stepped over me or on me take away the love that God has put inside of me. I did not allow them to take the light that God has shined through me but instead I allowed it to make me a better person as I pray for all the things of God.

I am so blessed to be able to sit here and tell you my life story and I am blessed to be in the place that I am in. I acquired a to series on OMNI television after they saw my Facebook live show where I talked about issues I found important and I began interviewing local government officials and politicians.

My television series Island Tea with Althea is broadcasted all around Canada and I'm now in my second year with my TV show. I've interviewed people that I never thought possible and I was recommended to run for MLA (Municipal Legislative Assembly) by Minister Miranda, minister of education. I sat down with Sandra Jensen, minister of infrastructure and I also sat down with the CEO of the chambers of Commerce. I have even interviewed the mayor of Calgary, the premier of Alberta, for my TV show.

I've accomplished so much although many people told me that I wasn't going to amount to anything and that I wasn't good enough to do half of the things I've done. By the grace of God I'm still standing and I'm now signed on to my second year of my TV show. I've interviewed huge Jamaican artists and I realized I am a character that can't be bought.

A Man

A good man makes you want to be a better woman. It took thirty-eight years of my life to understand how to be loved, how to love someone, and what it is to be loved. Based on my knowledge of love I thought loving someone was having sex all the time. I have confused sex with love eighty percent of my life, not realizing that love is patient and understanding.

There is great intimacy involved between couples and I did not understand that when someone loves you it is more fulfilling to be held all night with that one person, rather than having twenty minutes of intercourse. Along my journey I also realized how important it is to have a spiritual connection with your husband, your spouse or whoever you choose to live your life with.

We live in denial of love and we live in a sexual world instead of a more emotional or spiritual world and another thing I learnt in my journey is that we cannot keep love alive. Without the guidance and the spirituality effect of God in our lives, it is impossible to keep love alive, especially without the covenant of God. It will only last so long if it's sexual, there has to be a more spiritual bond.

It is this spirituality that endures eternally and it is the spirituality that leads you to connection. It makes sense to me now at this time of my life that the sexual aspect is a gift from God for us to enjoy each other but it's not the most important aspect of a relationship. I have wasted so much time looking for love in all the wrong places.

I've now entered into a spiritual connection, a physical connection and an emotional connection and I have learnt from my prior relationships that nothing can survive without respect and trust. A relationship or marriage is made up of ingredients and if one ingredients is lacking in the relationship then the relationship crumbles.

It's almost like baking a cake and if you forget to put in an ingredient in the cake it's ok but it's not at its full potential. I just needed to share this with my readers because I've put myself through so much sadness and hardship looking for these ingredients.

If you weren't taught these things and if you weren't raised with a man or a father in your life to show you how you should be treated as a woman, as a lady, as a young lady you don't adapt to these. If my story could just make a change in one person's life I would have done my job. I feel it's selfish for me to know and feel these things and not share it with the world.

Self-hate is damaging, it is one of the worst things that you could ever have or feel about yourself. I'm at a place in my life where I haven't looked in a mirror in a very long time. I put my clothes on to go outside, to go to a dance or to have something to drink and I'm very fidgety. I'm asking everyone if I look ok every minute. I feel uncomfortable in my skin, and as if everything about me is wrong.

I took this from my mind and I brought it into my heart and that's a struggle itself. When you take information and put it into your mind if your mind is strong enough you can release the negativity but if your mind is not, then you make negativity in your heart and it's so much harder to remove the self-hate.

As I look at my journey, I realize that to hate yourself is to hate God and to hate the people around you, including your brothers and sisters. Each and every one of us is a part of God and if you don't love yourself, how can you love God and how can you love the people in your life?

It's like making an allowance for the family in your home and when you make that allowance for your family and friends you're able to make allowance for other people that are not in your surroundings.

Nothing gets better with self-hate and I realize that and I learnt that over time. I had to lose a lot of things and a lot of people in my life to get to know me and to understand me – that's where self-love begins.

9

Purpose

I'm ready to reopen another business so I chose to open another salon, it seemed like I always go back to what I know. In 2007, I opened *Differenz Trenz Salon & Spa*. This time I knew a little better about owning a business and business management. I finished my hairdressing certificate and got my Journeyman's license as a hairstylist, I also went to the DeVry Institute of Technology Career College and took business operations.

I had a plan and I had dreams, not knowing my plan might shift. I found the space which was 1700 ft², found an investor and things looked brighter and I got three hundred and fifty thousand dollars from the investor to open my place. It looks the investor felt sorry for me because he never took back a dime from me and he gave me more money than I have ever seen.

I invested in houses and cars, I was living large. I owned three house all at once and had over one hundred thousand in the bank. I could buy what I wanted and do what I wanted, so I opened my salon. It took some time to get off but I worked hard until I made a name for myself in the barber salon industry.

My shop was opened from 2007 – 2018. I had some up's and down's, good times and bad times, but honestly, I loved my salon. The passion I had for it was unexplainable. When it was busy, my eyes would light up and all I could do inside was say thank you to God over and over.

I felt a sense of achievement, a million times over. I only did lady's hair at the time and then there was a large market for men cuts and barbering. Things were slow because I had a barbershop next door to my store and they would take every male customer that came around since they already built up a clientele and they also brought in a hairdresser and a nail technician. It was hard. I was fighting my culture again and I was trying to stand tall. I held on for some years.

One day someone brought a little Jamaican man into my shop. He had just come from Jamaica on a work permit but was not working. It was to help him come to Canada and he was sitting in his people house doing nothing looking out the window day after day.

At the time it was like he was a hidden treasure no one knew and they would not give him a chance so I took the chance on him. He went to different places to get a job but nobody hired him so he had heard something about me and somebody brought him in.

I put him under my wing and treated him as if he was my son. He had a little baby girl and I grew to love her very much, more than anyone knows. I took care of them and was good to him, as good as I was to my own children.

However, he became disrespectful to me when the same people that didn't want him were telling him that his chair was waiting for him. They realized that he had a great skill and that he was talented and so he lost all respect for me. It seemed as though he wanted the shop for himself or as though I didn't deserve it.

I made him what he is, I went out in the snow to bring him, customers and at the gym to bring him customers, but he wasn't appreciative, he was arrogant and acted like I was working for him.

I decided I have to make some serious changes. He was a great barber (no one can take that from him) but he was a terrible businessman. His heart changed toward me and at times I hated him for losing trust and faith in me. We could have being a great team but he does not believe in teamwork and wanted to be a one-man show. He even said that to me in my place of business but I hope he learns that this is not how business works. You can see a man's face but not is heart.

That chapter of my life with him is closed. I felt he became toxic like the community he was in, now he's at the barbershop he wanted to beat and I have moved on to bigger and better things. I don't surrounds myself with negative people anymore, so if you are not uplifting me you need to remove yourself from my environment.

Moving into the purpose of my life, I ran my salon for 11 years. I started it from scratch but it was now time to close this door so that I could have room to open the new doors. I don't have the same passion nor love for the salon, in fact it actually repulses me. I hated being in there, I hated being around the customers, I hated being around the staff and I hated the area and the people, I knew it was time to close the door.

I had no love for my salon left. I was finding bowls in the ceiling of my salon with mice poop and there was no explanation. No one knew anything and it was scary, so it was time for me to remove myself from danger.

It was not fun anymore and there was power working against the salon, it was time to leave. I was there for eleven years, from 2007 to 2018 and never saw these things but they must have been there to hinder my salon. So the door was closed so that new doors could be opened and I've been working on a different business plan.

I wrote a chapter in a book called "I'm a brilliant woman volume 3" and I believe I was one of ten authors who did not get any money from the book but it led me to this book, so from small things big things will grow. We are in the book but he publisher got all the credit. It was a learning process. You can find that book online.

They used my married name (Powell) but no one knows me by that name. Nevertheless, it gave me a chance to write this book and everything has to start from somewhere. In 2018 it was the number one bestseller and amazingly the money for the book was donated to abusive women.

I have started my second year on the TV show Island Tea with Althea on OMNI ROGERS. I've poisoned all the bad weeds and started with fresh grass and I'm now able to focus on my purpose. I realize what my purposes is and I'm here to inspire, educate, inform and embrace in law and love.

It was a very difficult decision to let go of the store. There was a lot of panic, sadness and anger. I felt so much emotions but one day it finally came down to starting moving stuff out in my car piece by piece. I wanted to control my situation because I didn't want anybody else to control it for me, so I prayed, meditated and then took charge of it.

I wanted to be out of there more than anything else in the world and so that final chapter of my life with Differenz Trenz is closed. I thought I wouldn't survive, and I know that most people in the world feel that way but don't let fear hold you down or cripple you. Don't get attached to material possessions, they come and go.

You may have been attached to it for years and when that happens it is one of the hardest thing to let go, but sometimes you have to know how to let go, so that other doors can open. Better things are waiting for, you have to let go and you have to close doors in order to open other ones and that was my problem, I couldn't see that far.

I now look with the eyes of God instead of looking with the eyes of men and when I did that I began to see the world in a different way. I have interviewed government officials from all over as well as International artists from around the world and I just began. I'm planning to turn the show into the number one International TV talk show of Canada and I have no plans of stopping.

I know now what my purpose is and I'm learning to love people and the things around me. I'm trying to build lasting relationship of love in my immediate family, with my husband and with my brothers and sisters because if I can't love them on the inside I can't love anybody on the outside.

At this moment I am working on my family for 2019. I'm working on my children and my husband because I have quite a bit of broken pieces. My purpose now is to put my family first, make my home strong and give my life to God and I know that everything that I've set myself out for will be put in place.

I had an opportunity to run for MLA In the government but me chose not to run because I was worried. I was scared and I carried a fear that they would dig into my background and people would destroy me. Its politics and it's nasty. People lose their characters and they use people to do anything to win but I'm a little bit disappointed that I allowed fear to make me back off. I should not continue and allow fear to distract me but there are greater things to come.

What God has for you and what he has for me, no one can change. As long as God is above, there will be another time, another opportunity and believe you me I will take this opportunity to run in the government to make a difference in the community and in world leadership.

My purpose is to share information to strengthen women and men all around the world and to share my story with them to let them know that anything is possible if you strengthen your spirituality and your mind. When you do this, it is impossible for anything to stop you.

Peace is an important ingredient of life. Find peace and joy in everything that you to do and hold on tight to God, because he never lets you down. No matter what you are going through, he always has you, so learn to hold on.

I am now living in my purpose. What a blessing it is to have come from a place where people did not value me or respect me not did they did not think very much of me. They did not want to sit with me nor eat with me and they thought that I was less than what I am.

I have encountered some difficult times, but somewhere along the road I have grown into my purpose. I started with a Facebook live TV show Called Sunday Tea with Althea. I came up with that show from a girl that I was mentoring in my hair salon. I always said God puts people in our lives for a reason and a season.

He placed this young lady in my life in 2017. She wrote me a letter and sent it to me on Facebook messenger and the letter told me of how much she appreciates me and how much she values the things that I am talking about on Facebook. She spoke about how she would love for me to take her under my wings and teach her, the skill of owning a business and she said that she looked up to me.

I was in a really low place in my mind until I received that message. I didn't understand what I was doing, where my life was going or what was I here for (my purpose). I just had so many empty spaces in my mind, my heart and my stomach; unexplainable things but I know the words that she used that day lifted me up.

Her words showed me that I was capable of saying good things and capable of speaking positively and that I could make changes in others' lives, positive changes. I returned her call and we spoke for a while on the phone. She told me that she admired me and would love to grow up to be just like me and that's amazing to hear all those things from someone.

We talked and talked and she said she took hairdressing in the United States. She's now in Canada with her family and would love to continue her hairdressing. So like I always do, I didn't say NO and that's one of my faults. I never say no to anyone, I always want to help and so I said yes, come on in and we were pretty close for a little while, not a very long while but a little while.

Sometimes people come to you for their reasons and their purpose not knowing that they came to open a door for you. The door that she opened was a door to my purpose and the door to open and inspire changes in the lives of millions. Even though she came for her own reasons, she came to open a door for me as well.

The door that was opened was that I was a great talker and I continued to do this little talk show and on Facebook not knowing how far it would take me. Remember that little things are the beginning of great things. I did know the number of people I would meet through this journey; and I did not know where this would go.

It was kind of funny, exciting and cool to be talking through your phone and having people replying through text, that's what I mean, it's crazy what technology can do nowadays. One thing led to another and my views started going from five hundred a week to one thousand and then from One thousand to two thousand and then to four thousand.

It started growing and exceeding my expectations and one thing led to another. She came to me and said, "I heard that they're looking for a patois TV show" and it was either the girl or her friend that introduced me to The TV station Omni Rodgers and she said that I would be amazing.

There was a spot available. I never thought much about it. I started talking to my friends and my friends reminded me that seven years ago I wanted to be a talk show host, and that that was what I was good at (talking) so I just took it for what it was. I persisted a little further and had a meeting with this gentleman.

I said to him, "I heard that you guys are looking for a show and that a slot is available, what I would have to do to get in?" He then told me that I had to do a pilot but I didn't know what a pilot was, I thought it was a man that flew the plane. I couldn't really begin to think what that word meant.

I got a meeting with them and figured out what a pilot was and what we had to do. The thing about it was that he wanted thousands and thousands of dollars for this pilot and I didn't know where I was going to get the money but I just kept my faith and my hope and I continued to pray that maybe I'd be able to give two hundred dollars and there.

We just decided we're going to do this pilot and I was paying him two hundred dollars through money transfer so that I could keep the receipts because you never know what could happen. As we went further and further the pilot was done, we made it. It was based on Caribbean people and the Caribbean dance, culture and experience.

He sent me a copy of it before he sent it into the TV station and I was just amazed. I very was happy and that was the start of my purpose. In the midst of all my glory, it showed me that nothing stays the same. Now, the same young lady that wanted to be me, turned against me and became disrespectful, but I feel as if she has served her purpose.

While she is being busy hating me, I'm being thankful for her opening doors for me. That's why I say that people come into your life for a reason and a season. You must allow your journey to continue because there is always a lesson involved. The new lesson that I learnt is that in all business transactions is to cover myself.

The pilot show was filmed and then they charged me, he was trying to steal my show from me. He said the people from Omni, and Rodger was busy and didn't have time to meet with me. I wanted the CRTC NUMBER in my own name and he delayed me.

I set up a discreet meeting with the director and then had them email him and cc me. He called me and gave me the wrong time of the meeting, showing his true character but I ended up at the meeting a few hours earlier so that I had a chance to meet, greet and talk with everybody. I also brought a few people with me to ask questions for me so that I would not get angry or out of content.

They were able to put him in his place, and it was better for me to show professionalism and the end of the day I got what I wanted. I got my CRTC number, shown in my name and the broadcasting number in my name. By the time we left the meeting and went back to my place of business. I received a phone call from the video guy telling me that he wanted to sit down and talk with me.

I gave him the green light and he showed up. He told me that my friends embarrassed him by asking inappropriate questions about the contract and he was busted, for trying to frame and impersonate me and trying to steal.

He looked at me and said that the business deal was no longer valid and that he would still shoot the show with a twenty thousand dollar fee for the year and he said that I would have to pay it in increments every three months.

I humored him told him and told him that I was going to give him a deposit knowing that I had no intention of giving him a dime. He was taking me for a ride, or so he thought. I spoke to the manager and got the CRTC number contract of the show in my name and he was removed from me. People come into your life for a reason and season.

10

Miracles

My chapter of miracles. There has been so many miracles that have happened in my life and I can't forget them. They seem to come when I'm at my lowest point. My biggest miracle is that I'm alive today and I give God the grace and the thanks, that I'm able to share my life's journey with many people around the world. I've been through some difficult times and I've always said to myself that I have to continue to do good to everyone around me.

I have such great memories of my son Chris. I remember one time I was driving in the car with my son, one of my miracle children and there was a man in the middle of the road begging for money I remember getting agitated with that man and my son looked over at me and said mom, "You have to be careful how you treat people, that man could have been a test he could have been your season or your reason.

I didn't look at it that way. He got me thinking, so I dug deep in my pocket and searched all over the car just to find a dollar or something just to give to this man, because when my son put it in those terms I knew that he was right. He said, "You never know if that could have been God or someone to change your life", so I know that my son is special.

He taught me such a great lesson that day, now, I can never see somebody and not give to them. My second blessing and lesson is my second daughter.

What a blessing, she came at a time in my life when I needed her more than anything else in the world and even though I couldn't see it at that time she proved it to me.

When she talks about me she talks about me with admiration. She tells me everything that she is, is because of me and she reassures me of my strength and how special I am. Even when I feel like I'm down-and-out and I can't go another step further, she always knows how to see bigger than what I can see. She always looks at me and says, "Mommy Use the eyes of God and not the eyes of humans.

She reminds me that I am special and that God has a great mission and plan for me. There are miracles! How can I not be blessed? Each and every one of my life's' miracles have taught me how special I am, how to cry, how to love and how to forgive.

I remember when my son was about five years old he looked at me and said, "Mommy you know what I want for Christmas?" I asked him what he wanted and he said, "I would love to have you and daddy in the same place for Christmas." All he ever wanted was family. My miracle son stood by me and promised me that he would never leave me until he was sure that there was somebody who would love me as much as he loved me, and he held to his promise.

When I think of my life, I see how blessed I am. I am highly favored by the good Lord above and I embraced the billions of people that will hear my words, have my words strengthen their mind and their inner self; save them from their dark time, strengthen their spirits and help them to find peace from within.

I want to let people know that miracles begin from God and within ourselves and this process starts with self-love. More than anything in the world God knows that the loss of my children could break me and I was faced with the loss of my child but God so loved me and covered me. He covers us under his blood.

This is another miracle for me, and this miracle has left my heart to surrender to God. It has left me loving and passionate in a way that I never thought I could love and it has left me wanting to live every single day as if it was my last. I don't want to miss a second and I don't want to miss an hour.

I want to see everything from the morning until night. I wake up thankful but I have to share these things with the world because I know it's possible to be at peace with yourself, your environment and your surroundings. I am full of gratitude. I get such a moment's now, just like the one that told me to say thank you to GOD for covering my son and for saving my son who was in accident when his car was in a ditch when it rolled over.

Another thought that came to me, was his step mother or grandfather that I spoke about in one of my chapters. She died last year. They had a strong connection I know she saved him in the accident. She held him and he explained that he felt a hand on him holding him. All of this was just the spirit of God working through all of us.

Another friend that had a close connection with my son's stepmother told me that she had a dream about her and she told me the same thing I thought which is that she was holding on tight to my son. She so for the rest of my life I will dedicate my life to helping others and making a better life for people around the world.

I am also so thankful for all the people in my life, my brothers, sisters and nieces and I am thankful for who they are. I would not change one of my family members because they are unique and my gift from God.

Another remarkable miracle was chosen in love through God. It was time for me to find the love of my life and to have God choose the man of my life. I put it in my head and I decided it's time to be married. It was time to find somebody to share my life with physically mentally and spiritually and it was going to take God to send someone in my life and I opened my mind and my heart for these changes.

I knew that every woman deserves a man to love them and I believe in my heart and soul that God has made a partner for every person but sometimes we just have to wait on God. I decided to put myself out there so I could find my blessing and my miracle and its funny how God sends people into your life.

So as I run my salon and hire barbers from time to time, I hired a new barber and he was a tall handsome man. I asked him, "Do you have anybody that's as handsome as you that is a good hard working man that would make a woman proud?" I believe I said it jokingly not sincerely and within seconds he flipped his phone open and showed me one picture.

It was like God-sent that one man for me because he didn't open his phone and say do you like him or him instead he just stuck with one guy he thought about and said, "I have somebody that's an amazing person and he would be so great for you."

I took a look at the picture and I was in intrigued so I said I would like to see a better picture because you know us all kind of look at men for looks and the picture that I saw didn't look too good. However, he sent me a different picture and it was nice. I thought about it, this time I didn't want looks, I wanted somebody who was going to love me for who I am and would love them for who they are.

I wanted someone that would respect me and I would respect him and we were going to have a spiritual connection with God. These are the things that I started to see and value. It wasn't so much about the sex anymore because I was one of the most confused person when it came to sex and love. I had to separate the two.

We started talking on the phone for very long time back and forward and he sounded very genuine. He have this peacefulness in his voice but I had never met him. Looks could be deceiving but I felt something that I had never felt before and it drew me closer and closer to him. Even when I said to myself that this was crazy you can't like someone that you don't know and you don't want to hear somebody all the time that was what I wanted.

I would rush home at nights to hear his phone call and I would wake up in the morning because he was going to phone me. I couldn't wait for the phone call and this continued to happen for months and months. I laid in my bed and I listened to him night after night day after day and finally I had to make the decision that it was time to meet.

I was scared to death and he was all the way in Jamaica. I didn't know much about that place I didn't have anybody that I really knew there. I had to take a trip all the way to the Caribbean to a man that I've never met but I was intrigued.

Part of me said, "No don't be stupid," and the other part of me said "just leap. "I've always been a spontaneous person so I leaped. I remember going to the airport and taking the plane. I can't tell you how I felt I was sitting on that plane as I was trying to go through a hundred different scenarios.

I thought, "what am I going to say, how am I going to say it, I'm not going and look at him, maybe a kiss him on his forehead, maybe wait a week for him to kiss me and lots more. I didn't know him that's for sure but if he was going to respect me, we are not going to have sex.

I went through so many different scenarios the excitement was killing me I was intrigued and I felt young and vibrant it was like Stella got her groove back. I landed in the Caribbean and it was hot, my hair flew up and I walked out and grabbed my bag. I was going really slowly because I was very scared but I was also excited. I can explain the emotions that and felt for him but they feel so good and yet so scary.

I continued to walk but nobody realized that I was on cloud nine, they could have stolen my suitcase and I wouldn't have known. I've never seen that much black people in my entire life and I'm a black woman, and I've never seen that much black people in one place. I was amazed and all this emotion was overwhelming.

When I walked outside of the airport I didn't have to look over, I knew who he was immediately and from the look that he gave me I knew he was going to be the man or husband that I would be with for the rest of my life or at least I would try.

The way that he looked at me was absolutely captivating and it's so strange that every person in my family seemed to take to him. I remember the day of our wedding it was amazing we were 90' above sea level and I was upstairs getting dressed along with his mother, my sisters and my best friend was there also. Everybody just looked so amazing and were happy for me.

I was doing my hair and my best friend ran upstairs, she flew from Canada to Jamaica just to be there for me. When she got up the stairs she came to me that she said that it was the end of the world. I asked her why she said such a thing and she asked me to open the curtain and look at the sky.

The sky went from beautiful blue to the darkest sky I've ever seen in my life with frost and rain and I was devastated. I thought that I was not supposed to marry this man since the world seems like it was coming to an end but within the time I was finished getting dressed the sky opened up and it was the most beautiful as blue sky.

Then the rain started to drizzle down on him and I stooped at the window 90' above looking down at him standing there waiting patiently. I just had the feeling and I knew it was right and it was time for me to get married. My mother held on to my hand, my son looked at me and I grabbed the tail of my dress and I had twelve of the most important people in my life walk me down the aisle.

My mother had my tail and my son had my hands. My feet trembled and my hands shook and my son squeezed me. I said, "Mom it looks right and you know it feels right, "then I just walked. I've never had a man in my life look at me the way he looked at me and I remember just before I stepped down he left his post and he came and got me from the staircase.

All I could see was tears in his eyes and I remember saying to him, "thank you for being the man that God has made you to be." He is such a humble man and that is what I wanted, a man that had that passion for me and when he looked at me it was so strong that he would cry.

I walked up to him on that ledge overlooking the ocean in the mountain and I looked at him and I said yes, he took me in his hands and I became his wife. From the day that I became his wife we have had some struggles and rough times but with the grace of God and the coverage of God we fight through it and that's my miracle.

Six months ago I was at home, I had a meeting with an advertising agent so she came to my home and we went out on the balcony to have a chat. It was such a nice sunny day, we came to an agreement about the advertisement and then I decide to walk her outside. I looked at him and said, "there is rain on my car, your car and the walk side but no one else's' drive way had rain or was even wet.

I ask her if she saw what I was seeing and she said yes. I walked to the step in front of my house and I could feel rain and it was falling on my property. I was confused so I decided to check the neighbor's driveway to see if it was raining but it was only over my home, what a blessing.

I have felt it with the wind when while every tree was still on my block but my tree was blowing like crazy and the tree was a pine tree which never shook. It was miracle after miracle.

My last miracle was when I was sleeping in bed and three angles came to in the dream. They showered me with dust the most beautiful colors that I have ever seen red, gold and blue. Some looked like stars from the sky and when the angles sprinkled it on me it was one of the most peaceful feelings. I was happy and content and then they started to disappear. I was begging them to stay but they said that I would be ok and that I was covered and blessed and I woke up feeling very blessed.

11

Living to Inspire

I have some goals and plans that I have to put in motion. I remember a nursing home in Jamaica that took care of my grandmother and I believe it saved her even if it was not the best conditions. It has been a dream of mine to go back one day and rebuild the nursing home, supply them with clothes, bed sheets and pillow cases and medication.

I would like to teach women from all over the how to love themselves how be at peace with themselves and how I have overcome self-hate. I was the woman that hated myself could not look in a mirrors always hoping for the worst out of life, but I have found the secret of a successful life and it is loving yourself and God, and that changes all things.

I am at a place in my life now that I can inspire and help to make changes in others but not without them wanting it. I wanted the change so badly that I would have died for it and I wanted to be a better person because there was no peace in my life without me changing my life.

I have been there and it seemed so hard for the older folks in that nursing home. Some of them don't have children to visit them or take care of them. There were so many older people that lost their legs or arms it was the saddest thing I have ever seen and I just wanted to help them in any way that I could.

I remember when I went to see grandma I was so excited, I couldn't wait to see her. When I opened the gate to the nursing home, I noticed that there were all kind of dogs in the yard and it did not seem as if it was in the best condition. There was so many older people that had no legs some had no arms and it was sad for me to see older people like that, as it must have been sad for them.

You figure that when you get to be seventy or eighty years old it is time for you to get your best care or live your life without worries, but in this nursing home that did not seem to be the case. People were taken there and to left to die, including my grandma.

It seemed as if her children gave up on her, or maybe they could not afford to take care of her financially or maybe medication was too expensive, I am not sure as to what the circumstance was. I call it the dead yard, because that's what it was, no one ever went back home when they get there but just seem too died there.

I was looking for her and when I finally found her, she was lying in a bed all curled up in a ball so tiny and frail. All that I could do was to start crying and drop to my knees. I remember the nurse saying that they did not know she had kids because no one come to see her. I can't understand how her children could be so mean and hateful to their own mother.

I was devastated because there was no explanation for such an act especially when you have given birth to that much kids. Immediately I picked her up in my arms and started to rock her to comfort her while tears were running down my eyes. I remember seeing tears running down her face as she cried out for her last daughter saying that her kids left her alone and threw her away.

She was almost fully blind and I kissed her on her face so she could feel the warmth of my lips on her forehead and the affection of another human love. However, she had no idea who I was and that was one of the most painful and heart breaking things that has ever happened to me, to see her in that state.

I loved her and I was sorry for what her kids had done to her. If I could change it I would. The pain I felt seeing her like that left me hoping that she would die and go to heaven with God because she deserve so much better .

I remember having my driver take me to the supermarket and I bought her some oil for her hair and sweet and oranges, it was her favorite and I bought treats for all the elderly people in the nursing home. I bathed her, brushed her beautiful hair that was white as snow and changed her bed sheets. Then I shared the sweets with all the others.

I held her in my arms as if she was my little baby and it was very special for me to have that time with her as it was going to be the last time that I saw her. She was about 101 years old, no one knew for sure and she died a year after. I felt a peace that she was not by herself anymore and that she was under the wings of the angels and God.

My mother has had a hard time since because she was living in Canada where my mom took care of her mother but she was so lonely that she asked us not to let her die in Canada. She wanted to go home and so we grant him her wish. It is my duty to make sure that nursing home stays open because it looked after great elderly people that has nowhere else to go and die, even if it is not the best I loved miss Violet Merrick with all my Heart and I dedicate this book to her.

It is very important that I put the effort into bringing back this saving Violet nursing home. I have learnt that we must help in life because what goes around will definitely come back around and these are the things in life that we should be sure to do. Each and every one as a journey and everyone must die so let be good to each other's while we are here on earth.

What I learnt from this situation is to forgive each other so that we can free ourselves from all the negative emotions. That is my responsibility, to take care of my parents in their older years when they get frightened, as they get older and as they turn back into children. It is the rule of life, it is our job to treat each other with love and understanding and turn hostility into compassion. I am grateful to be able to share my life story with the world.

As a talk show host on television, I remind people that dreams can come true when we have the courage to believe in ourselves. The path is not easy but it is worth it. In writing about my journey I trust that I will inspire you to never give up. For many years, I was an angry woman but I have learned over the years how my words and emotions can have a devastating impact and the ability to either elevate or destroy my children's relationship with me.

My daughter, my *wash belly baby,* meaning my last child has felt the bulk of my angry words, words meant for her father but directed at her. There came a time when I caught myself, and I realized the true impact I had on the daughter I am supposed to love and protect. Instead, I would lose my mind when I was with her father. My behavior was unbelievable. To put my trust in a human instead of God, was the first mistake I made. We need to know ourselves, to understand ourselves and know our purpose in life. I often felt like an empty corpse walking around, *soulless*.

Eventually I realized that not only was my daughter a princess and a blessing but she saved my life in many ways. My youngest daughter once asked me why her skin was darker than mine, she believe her skin wasn't as beautiful and I told her that the melanin in her skin was her MAGIC .This story was printed and covered by CBC. This is her story, a legacy left for her to carry on down to her kids. Sometimes when God gives us things in our lives, we need to understand they are there for a purpose and a reason some come to save, destroy, and teach but most importantly to show us how to love.

I was living a life consumed with hate and anger. It swirled and spiraled touching everything and everyone around me. But in order to make changes I would have to lose friends and family. I had to be in a lonely place to get to know me without any distractions.

When I think of my old self, my sad, unhappy and looking for love self, I realized that I was always searching for it from external sources. Some days I would look in the mirror and I wouldn't see beauty. I'd see a stranger staring back at me, so I'd go searching for something material to define who I am.

When I was with my daughter's father, I allowed him to make me feel like I wasn't worth loving and it was the worst feeling some could ever have because you forget to please yourself and trying to please a person rather than yourself, can make you feel unworthy of being respected and treated with decency.

After all this, my daughter still worshipped the ground he walked on which wish made me twice as angry with her, so I carried this anger towards him, towards her and most of all towards myself for allowing someone to take so much away from me.

I lost the ability to trust those closest to me and it was a struggle every day to not let these experiences diminish my drive. After all that I've experienced I realize that life is here for you to make mistakes and learn from them, use these mistakes to make better choices.

Life is a lesson, life is about learning. When you stop learning, you stop living. Have faith. As human beings, we are constantly looking for validation from others but with these changes in my life I feel stronger and happier because I realize to live a good life is to live one full with learning from your mistakes. Learn to love and value yourself. I am not my past and I am not my past mistakes, but they have led me to a great destiny, so please don't define me by my past.

THIS IS MY QUADRANT
THIS IS HOW I MAKE IT THROUGH THE DAY

THIS IS MY CIRCLE

Spirituality

Affirmations

Meditations

Health

Eat Properly

Exercise

Sleep (helps you to grow strong)

Mentor

Find someone who can be a source of instruction

Spiritual Mentor

Ask God for someone who can guide you spiritually as to what God desires for your life

START SOMETHING SIMILAR, FIND WHAT MAKES YOU STRONG

DESIGNED BY:
ALTHEA CLARKE

Love Letter To God

I would like to send God a love letter and this is how it begins:

Dear God,

Thank you for my mother and thank you for my brothers and my sisters. Thank you for being my saving grace, thank you for teaching me patience in all my circumstances and situations and thank you for giving me the strength and energy to put my story down on paper to share it with the universe, to release all shame and quilt. Thank you for the transformation in me and for making me whole again. May this book touch each and every one with the blessing and miracle of God.

.

APPRECIATION TO MY MOTHER

Love Peace Joy. .... Thank you mama for the nine months that you carried me. You are my strength you are my rock and you are my fortress, When I think of how hard you have worked to support us it bring tears to my eyes. When I see the strength in you, it makes me want to fight harder for life, and harder to make you proud of me you want my special person.

You really are special. I have seen you overcome so many things and I've seen you overcome nervous breakdown by yourself without a pillar or a doctor and that is what I consider strength. I have seen you lose brothers and sisters and bounce back and I've seen you lose the most important thing in your life (your mother). It almost left you crippled but you came back strong to take care of us.

We were never hungry, you were never dirty and we always had a roof over head and no matter what your situation was, you have always put us first. I don't remember ever seeing a man kiss you because you had so much respect for your daughters in the house. You wouldn't allow us to see anything that you thought would clutter our minds and I thank you mama, you are a brilliant woman.

Thank you for taking the opportunity come over to Canada to give all of your children the opportunity to have a chance at a better life. Thank you for working out in the cold in -50 and 40 degree at the time just so that you can send food and money for us. Thank you for clothing, educating me and thank you for the strength that you've given me.

If they think of taking you away from me mama I will search all through the world and cross the ocean to find you momma. I wouldn't change you for the world. I dedicate every success in my life to you, you are an amazing individual, and Mamma by the grace of God when this book is printed and published, I will be that daughter that sits by your bed and I would read this to you, because there's no person in the world who deserve all the wonderful things in the world than you.

I am proud that you're my mother. I don't care if you're rich or poor and I don't care if you're white or black I'm just glad that you're just my mother. I don't take enough time out in the world to let you know how important you are and how amazing you are. Yes Mamma I have seen you work, I have seen the pain in your face and I could also feel the pain in your heart, but no matter whatever happened all nine of us was always fed.

I will search the world for you. I would a travel beyond and back for you mama. You are a gem mamma. I am just so thankful that I'm your daughter and I'm also thankful that my cells and DNA are made up of you. You've been a mother and a father you've been a friend and the sister. You've been everything that I could ever want. I know that we've all grown up and we're living our own lives, but you are not taken for granted and you will never be forgotten mama.

I will feed you when you can't feed yourself , I' will change your clothes when you can't change your clothes , I will bathe you mama I will read you stories and I will not allow you to ever be alone. I love you with every ounce and every cell of my being and I thank you for life, I thank you for the family that you put me into and I thank you for heritage.

I just thank you mama and I am hoping that one day I'm able to give you the life that you deserve. I put these things out in the universe and I'm watching them manifest, so mama thank you for your wisdom and your strength. Thank you for your struggles, thank you for everything that you've taught me up until this day.

Thank you mama you for your guidance, you are my beginning and you will be my end. I love you mamma. Thank you with all the gratitude in the world. I thank and I thank God that you are my mother. I am so grateful for you. I don't tell you this enough but I write this for every woman around the world let your mother and your father know how great they are and that they deserve to know how wonderful and amazing they are. Let your mother know that her giving your life is a gift and you thank her dearly. Life is an amazing thing.

I pray that this book has been a blessing to you.
For more information on the author, please
contact us or visit her on:

Facebook:
https://www.facebook.com/ClarkeAlthea

Journal

_____

_____

_____

_____

_____

_____

_____

_____

_____

_____

_____

_____

_____

Made in the USA
Middletown, DE
26 February 2019